If you want to come alive, if you truly wa[...]
and meaning, you need to read this bool[...]
time as this.

The books I love, the books that change me, are the books written by someone who has lived faithfully and with integrity to the story they have written. That's why I love this book. Justin has lived every page in this book by giving his life to work that matters and allowing himself to be changed through the change he is trying to make in the world. Today there are so many people young and old dying on the inside, crushed by a culture of consumption and selfish ambition, but it doesn't have to be this way. Justin gives us a roadmap to break out of what's expected and to reorder, reinvent, and reimagine how your life can change the world, and he honestly shows us how God changes us in the process. Thoughtfully written through a life well lived, I am giving this book to my college-age sons because I believe it will help them discover what they were made to do, and I know it will do the same for you.

Despite the challenges in the world today, Justin Zoradi helps us remember who we are: bearers of light, called by God to risk, build, and inspire. Let this powerful book guide you on your own journey toward doing work that matters.

As we become more connected than ever, the problems in the world loom large and close, causing many of us to check out and attempt to survive the chaos. Justin's story and this book will help inspire and equip you in your journey of finding your place and making a true impact. In time such as these, *Made for These Times* will encourage you to not just survive but thrive.

A powerful message of living for a grander and greater purpose, *Made for These Times* will ignite your heart to love more deeply and respond more fully to the world around you. Justin's sage advice and vulnerability will equip you to lead a life of sustained service and outrageous love.

PETER GREER, president and CEO, HOPE
International; coauthor, *Rooting for Rivals*

Have you ever been overwhelmed thinking about how one person can ease the world's suffering? Confused by what, exactly, God is calling you to? If so, you could ask for no better guide than Justin Zoradi. He has devoted his career, and this book, to exploring how to fulfill our "insatiable desire to matter" by using our unique gifts to serve other people. Justin writes with great humility about the joy of self-forgetfulness in service of others.

LAURA TURNER, writer and journalist; contributor, *The Atlantic, Politco, The Washington Post, Slate,* and *Buzzfeed*

When Donald Miller and I launched the Mentoring Project, Don insisted, "We must hire Justin Zoradi. He's a beast." Don was right. Justin is a visionary leader, a creative starter with tireless work ethic, enthusiasm, and wisdom. Our explosive success growing the Mentoring Project from twenty mentors into a national movement is largely because of Justin's fire and skill. He can start anything and make it great. Read this book, and learn from one of the best.

JOHN SOWERS, president, the Mentoring Project;
author, *Fatherless Generation* and *The Heroic Path*

With wit and wisdom, Justin Zoradi shows us practical ways to help and heal a broken world. He's an important voice for our generation to hear.

SARAH THEBARGE, author; *The Invisible Girls* and WELL

How do you fuel the spark God's given you to change the world without burning out in the process? Justin is a trusted guide, whose wise insight can help you excel not only in what you are doing but, perhaps more importantly, who you are becoming.

JOSHUA RYAN BUTLER, author, *The Skeletons
in God's Closet* and *The Pursuing God*

I met Justin when I was nineteen, and he shaped the way I understand justice, vocation, and leadership. I'm so glad he packed all of his wisdom and experience on how to build, empower, and even let go of work that matters. This book will flip your life upside-down in the best way possible.

BRANDEN HARVEY, founder, the Goodnewspaper;
host, *Sounds Good Podcast*

I see a generation that wants to live on purpose, with purpose, for a purpose. And with *Made for These Times* we have a rallying cry and a field manual from a leader in Justin Zoradi who hasn't just written these words on doing work that matters; he's lived each one of them. That's not an overstatement. Justin is the real deal, and so is this book. Read it and be inspired.

PAUL ANGONE, author, *101 Questions You Need to Ask in
Your Twenties: (and let's be honest, your thirties too)*

These days it feels as if *fearful* and *cynical* are our default settings, but *Made for These Times* is an urgent reminder that God put us here and now for a reason. Justin Zoradi's story will inspire you, and his fantastic book will point you toward a life of purpose. Give it to the graduates in your life, and everyone else.

CHAD GIBBS, author, *Love Thy Rival, God &
Football,* and *Jesus Without Borders*

MADE
FOR THESE
TIMES

MADE FOR THESE TIMES

A START-UP GUIDE TO CALLING, CHARACTER, AND WORK THAT MATTERS

JUSTIN ZORADI

ZONDERVAN

Made for These Times
Copyright © 2018 by Justin Zoradi

Requests for information should be addressed to:
Zondervan, 3900 *Sparks Dr. SE, Grand Rapids, Michigan* 49546

ISBN 978-0-310-35107-8 (softcover)

ISBN 978-0-310-35539-7 (audio)

ISBN 978-0-310-35110-8 (ebook)

Published in association with D. C. Jacobson & Associates LLC, an Author Management Company www.dcjacobson.com.

Art direction: Curt Diepenhorst
Interior design: Denise Froehlich

First printing June 2018 / Printed in the United States of America

CONTENTS

"OPEN

YOUR EYES AND

SEE

WHAT YOU CAN

WITH THEM,

before they close

FOREVER."

———

ANTHONY DOERR

When Justin and I first met, in 2004, I was a twenty-year-old studying communications at Calvin College, and Justin and I both worked in the Student Activities Office under the mentorship of Ken Heffner. That year, Justin and I spent a lot of time helping to plan concerts and talking with students about the spiritual dimensions of pop culture. Soon into our friendship, I sensed that Justin would go on to do something big for the kingdom. He had already displayed great courage simply by moving from sunny California to the snow heaps of West Michigan. He was passionate about justice and believed that real-world problems and suffering required real-world action from God's people. As a sheltered Midwesterner cushioned by privilege, I had never experienced real injustice, but in conversation, Justin helped me to see it all around me. Further, he took the time to develop friendships in the office and outside of it. Even though Justin is only a few years older than I am, as a student I wanted to be like him when I grew up. (I'm not sure if that's happened yet.)

Nearly fifteen years later, my early premonitions about Justin have proven true. It's been a delight to see his non-profit, These Numbers Have Faces, grow over a decade and empower tens of thousands of promising young leaders in three African nations. And now, it's exciting to see Justin share his accumulated wisdom in the book you are holding. He's a living testament to the notion that our lives are not to be hoarded for ourselves, but to be poured out for others to bring life, freedom, and kingdom hope.

You probably picked up this book because you sense a stirring for something more. A more meaningful profession or vocation. A closer proximity to the marginalized. A deeper walk with Christ. Greater freedom to obey when he says, "Follow me." With personal anecdotes, biblical wisdom, and examples from history, Justin has offered a vision of that "more" life. It's not the life that our consumerist American culture holds out to us. Rather, it is the countercultural, upside-down life of the kingdom. As we say yes to God's call to partner with him in his plan of restoring all things, we will find the life of meaning, abundance, and peace that we are made for.

I believe that all of us were "made for these times." There's work that only we can do, relationships that only we can foster, brokenness that only we can help to mend. Justin has already spent his time on earth investing in "eulogy virtues"—the kind of actions that may not appear on a résumé but will be remembered at one's funeral. I'm excited to see the way that his book will unleash more of us to pursue those eulogy virtues, for the glory of God and the love of neighbor. So take up and read, anticipating that you will discover the "more" life you were made for.

KATELYN BEATY, author of *A Woman's*
Place: A Christian Vision for Your Calling
in the Office, the Home, and the World

Part I | THE AWAKENING

Chapter 1

HE DIDN'T LOOK UP

Sixteen hundred miles from California, I had moved to Michigan to start over. Proud to be one of the first of my friends from college to take the risk and leave it all behind, I signed up for the narrative of a young man striking out on his own but had failed to notice the fine print. When story became reality, I found myself alone, afraid, and in agony.

After settling in Grand Rapids, I'd be roused from sleep early in the morning with the faint sunrise peering in frost-covered windows. I would dress and slip out quietly into the chilly morning air, walking sometimes for hours at a time. In these quiet moments I'd catch whispers of a future, calling in a language I didn't quite understand.

In my new job at Calvin College, my boss, Ken Heffner, was the first to introduce me to a radical way of living in the world – one centered on service to others. He was a man of deep personal convictions, which he applied to every aspect of his life, from the mundane to the profound. This is where he believed real change in the world began. He used to say, "Nothing matters but the kingdom, but because of the kingdom, everything matters." At the time, I didn't know what he meant.

Under Ken's tutelage, I was learning and growing in abundance. My intellectual curiosity was on overdrive, and all the while I was sloshing through endless puddles of depression. I spent my evenings reading alone in coffee shops, smoking hopelessly on park benches, praying that someone, anyone, would come up and talk to me. The despondency only worsened when winter hit, and I found myself dragging a hair dryer on an extension cord to defrost the ice that had frozen my car doors shut. The bright skies of California were now faded postcards, colorless in the basement.

Taped to the wall of my bedroom in a house I shared off Franklin Street was that famous quote commonly attributed to civil rights leader Howard Thurman: "Don't ask what the world needs. Ask what makes you come alive, and go do that. Because what the world needs is people who have come alive."

The concept of coming alive was all well and good, and while my personal development was palpable, the feelings of loneliness were taking their toll. I was intellectually passionate about focusing my life on the concerns of others but had no practical outlet. Counting the months it had been since I'd received a physical hug from another person, I developed unique bursts of social anxiety, vertigo symptoms, and a bizarre case of acid reflux disease that had me vomiting almost daily.

Maybe I was just weak and physically unable to pursue

the convictions and theological underpinnings I aspired to. I feared I would be found out as someone who could talk the talk about doing amazing things in the world but lacked the chops to follow them up.

———

The snow had finally begun to melt when I met fifteen-year-old Malik on the crumbling curb in front of my house. Overweight and as depressed as I was, he approached bouncing a basketball, asking if I'd be up for some one-on-one. Malik lived with his grandmother two doors down. His dad had left before he was born, and his drug-addicted mother had been incarcerated for as long as Malik could remember. We built an odd friendship over the course of the next six months that normally began with his faint knock on my bedroom window at all hours of the day and night. We worked on projects around the house, he critiqued my cooking, and I taught him how to drive a stick shift in a nearby church parking lot. Our house kept the furnace on, and he could always find something in the fridge. We began spending most evenings together.

Malik's situation made my "problems" look tame. In many ways, we were exactly what the other person needed. He needed a mentor: someone to listen to him, affirm his insecurities, and give him a break from the chaos of life two doors down. At the same time, I think I needed a young man to mentor—someone to truly invest in and care for as opposed to merely contemplating the intellectual theories of compassion. My heart broke when he asked if he could come with me if I ever moved back to California.

One day, after unsuccessfully trying to visit his mother in prison, Malik came home and filled his stomach with a medicine-cabinet concoction. At fifteen, he'd simply had enough. My phone rang during work. It was David, his younger brother, who was hyperventilating. I prayed and cursed and prayed and cursed as I sped to the hospital. His stomach had been pumped hours before, and as I arrived they were putting Malik into a wheelchair to send him home. His eyes sunken and bloodshot, he gave me an embarrassed frown. He didn't like me seeing him like this, so weak and hollow. His attempted suicide devastated me to no end. It was clearly a cry for help. I went over to his house the next day and found him back in front of the television. He shrugged off my attempts at consolation, and we never spoke about it again.

The cards were stacked against Malik from the start. Born into a situation he couldn't change and an environment he couldn't escape, most days were bitter spoonfuls of hopelessness. My relationship with Malik, in its simple joys and depressingly dark lows, ignited in me a pragmatic sense of right and wrong, of justice and injustice. I began to understand the unseen benefits of middle-class privilege in contrast to the destructive web of inequality two doors down. I had a hard time fathoming that a young man born in the richest, most powerful country in the history of human civilization was unlikely to graduate from high school. The way Malik's life was headed, I began to worry he had a better chance of waking up each morning incarcerated than employed. But here he was, sitting on my floor, helping fold the laundry.

I worked for months trying to get Malik in a special program for kids with parents who are incarcerated. I met with after-school tutors and was unsuccessful at persuading him to attend service clubs, leadership trainings, and youth camps. I was putting in 90 percent and needed him to come the final ten. My strategy was loving and idealistic, but it was fueled by guilt at the same time. If only Malik had a hundredth of the attention, affection, and resources I'd been effortlessly handed from birth. But the years of front porch drug dealings and Doritos for dinner had taken their toll. Malik needed a reset button, a gigantic rubber eraser to wipe it all out and start fresh—a full restructuring of his entire world. I lay awake as sirens tore down the street; I prayed for Malik and pleaded with God for an answer.

My inevitable departure from Malik and Grand Rapids a few months later was terrible. Like everyone else in his life, I was now abandoning him too. My hard work at Calvin College paid off when I was introduced to a Presbyterian minister from Belfast, Northern Ireland, named Steve Stockman, who was in town promoting his new book about Irish rock legends U2. We hit it off almost immediately, and Steve offered me a job working for him in Belfast.

Malik tried to hide his disappointment as he helped me load up my black Hyundai hatchback. We hugged, a rare occurrence for us. He played it cool and boasted that he'd be playing varsity football next year, a fabrication we both knew was impossible. I promised we'd stay in touch as he closed the trunk, gave me a sad sideways glance, and lumbered down the driveway. As I drove past him heading for the freeway, I honked and waved. He didn't look up.

———

Ten years after I left Grand Rapids, I returned with my colleague Shoshon for a few meetings in western Michigan. Shoshon decided to rest for an afternoon at our hotel off 28th Street, so I took the car out to remember the city I once called home.

Without meaning to, I was drawn back to my old neighborhood and the house I used to rent off Franklin Street. I realized I was harboring a glimmer of hope that I'd run into Malik. I parked across the street, staring at his house and wondering if I was crazy. Would he still even be there? Would he remember? Would he even care? Maybe I had built our relationship up as something meaningful when, in fact, I was just another person who had come into his life and then left him behind. So I chickened out. No one appeared to be home, and I did not have the courage to knock. I actually felt relieved.

I still think about Malik. I've searched his name on social media for a clue of any kind. A few times a year I'll even scan the Grand Rapids obituaries online, worried I'll see his face. I'm not sure what I'm looking for or even what I want to find. All I know is that there's a certain guilt that lingers, the type that's ridden with cynicism and regret.

Was our relationship actually important? Did I do more harm than good?

In one of my first attempts at a pursuit larger than myself, I had failed massively. What if this path toward meaning, this hope that I was made for something more, was just a setup for disappointment?

Chapter 2

STARRY STARRY NIGHT

Actor Andrew Garfield was set to give his first public performance since graduating from a prestigious London drama school. He was cast as Ophelia in Shakespeare's *Hamlet* and would be performing at the original Globe Theatre in London.

In an interview with Brendan Busse from *America Magazine*, Garfield tracks back to this critical day in his career.

> "It's about two hours before and suddenly, I feel like I'm going to die," he remembered. "I genuinely feel that if I step on the stage I'm going to burn up from the inside out. I've never felt so much terror, like mortal dread, not-enoughness, self-doubt. Terror at being seen. Terror at revealing and offering my heart. Exposing myself, saying, 'look at me.'"[1]

To get some fresh air and calm his nerves, Garfield left the Globe Theatre to walk up and down the south bank of the River Thames. It was an overcast day, and his thoughts soon turned as dark as the London sky. "I begin thinking of throwing myself into the river. I have nothing to give, I have nothing to offer, I'm a fraud."

In this moment of intense pain, Garfield heard a familiar song. A street performer nearby was singing, rather badly, "Vincent" by Don MacLean. A bittersweet tribute to Vincent van Gogh, the classic song celebrates an artist plagued by equal parts genius and mental instability. But it was the imperfection of the performance that impacted Garfield most. "If that guy had stayed in bed saying 'I have nothing to offer, my voice isn't that good, I'm not ready to perform in public, I'm not enough.' If he had listened to those voices, I wouldn't have been given what I needed," he said. "His willingness to be vulnerable really changed my life."

This shared connection of artistic imperfection was a lifeline for Garfield, and it was where God met him on the banks of the Thames. "And literally the clouds parted and the sun came out and shone on me and this guy and I was just weeping uncontrollably. And it was like God was grabbing me by the scruff of the neck and saying, 'You've been thinking that if you go on stage you're going to die. But actually, if you don't go on stage you're going to die.'"

Garfield boldly returned to the Globe Theatre, put on a stunning performance, and would later go on to star in films like *The Amazing Spider Man*, *Hacksaw Ridge*, *Silence*, and *The Social Network*. He's received nominations for both an Academy Award and a Golden Globe.

Andrew Garfield's powerful experience on the River Thames reveals exactly why he *had* to become an actor. His micro story is a macro metaphor for all of us. He's been crippled by the penetrating fear we've all felt— the deep emotional ache that we aren't good enough, aren't smart enough, aren't courageous enough. Rather, we should throw ourselves in the river. Just like Andrew Garfield, it is this exact moment of despair where our journey begins. This is the place where the sparks of meaning and purpose begin to smolder. The pain is a pathway to our destiny.

———

If you're anything like me, you want to be good, you want people to like you, and you want to do important things. But on those certain dark days, inside you are a mess. You're insecure and anxious, with your self-confidence in the gutter. Some of us can even glimpse the life we want just up ahead, but we're handcuffed to comfortable habits that blur our vision, making it impossible to see the future clearly. It's in these moments that we find ourselves stumbling aimlessly into the gaping jaws of uncertainty, trying to bridge a chasm miles wide between the life we are living and the life God intends for us.

It was the final words of God to Andrew Garfield on the River Thames that hit me the hardest. Despite his terror, it wasn't the performance at the Globe Theatre that afternoon that would kill him. What would truly kill him was if he didn't do it at all. This is the ultimate tension. Will we die of the fear in finding our purpose, or will we die because we never find it at all?

If you've recognized this tension, good. That means you're awake to the high stakes at hand. We know we are built for more, but the prospect of discovering it is so abstract, so perilous, so confusing that we'd prefer to just live our lives on autopilot. As a result, we often feel as if we're sitting on the sidelines of our own life.

We are a culture of maximizers. We maximize points of joy and pleasure to minimize and avoid points of pain. We are a society so interconnected online and yet completely alone. We've normalized ordering food to our front door while we binge watch television all weekend. We long for intimacy and depth but so easily choose distraction and safety.

Made for These Times comes from a letter by Clarissa Pinkola Estes called "Do Not Lose Heart." It is a statement of both deep inspiration and sincere comfort for me. I believe now more than ever, these are the times for you to make a significant impact, whether it be in your family, your community, or around the world. The scope and scale don't matter. What matters is understanding how critical you are right now.

Don't forget, if you live in the global north and have a college degree, you are effectively a member of the most powerful people group the world has ever known. If you own a smartphone, you have a supercomputer in your pocket millions of times more powerful than all of NASA's combined computing when they put a man on the moon in 1969.[2] This isn't the time to tread water in the ocean of mediocrity. It is the time to leverage the unique point in human history you are privileged to be a part of.

Now, I don't believe in the myth of progress—that just by existing, over time human beings will eventually figure out how to solve problems and save the world. I believe, as Martin Luther King Jr. says, "Human progress never rolls in on the wheels of inevitability; it comes through the tireless efforts of people willing to be co-workers with God."[3]

For centuries, God has been putting these pieces together. Despite all the bad news you see on TV, I believe hundreds of millions of human beings have become co-workers with God to tackle the greatest challenges of our time. Despite the darkness in our world, within every tiny glimmer of hope is the hand of God clasped in partnership with the hands of human beings. In his genius and benevolence, God uses weak-kneed, distracted, and anxious humans to achieve remarkable things in their daily lives.

As we face the world's most pressing needs, it's easy to wish for the heroes of our history. People like Nelson Mandela, Rosa Parks, and Susan B. Anthony. As if somehow we could resurrect them from martyrdom, melt down the statues, snip out the date on the calendar in their honor, and bring them back to lead the charge for justice, equality, and sanity. Yet it is *we* who are called to these troubling times. Not Winston Churchill or Harriet Tubman, Frederick Douglass or Mother Teresa. It is *us* whom God has chosen for today.

This book is about why I believe you were made for these times and why I believe you've been given the perfect gifts to accomplish something incredible, big or small - in your own neighborhood or around the world. This book is for all types of people, but we all share a common virtue: we believe there has to be something more. There has to be a larger calling, a deeper meaning, a reason why we are here on earth for this short time with a beating heart and electricity in our veins.

You're reading this book because you've felt the inkling for something different. Things may look well and good to your friends and family, but inside you're just not satisfied. Unsettled. In my own life, it was a soft pinging, somewhere far away in the distance, like the sound of a hammer hitting a railroad stake miles away in the darkness. Faint, but relentless. I'd try and distract myself or retreat from the sound, but in the quiet of late nights or early mornings it rang true. It was this sound, mere echoes of a journey not yet chosen, that would wake me up in Michigan, driving me toward God and a relationship with Malik. The pinging has continued since.

In *Traveling Mercies*, author Anne Lamott describes the way in which Jesus pursued her like a cat, loitering around her house, trying to get in. It would follow her around, nudge her to pick it up, and it was always there at her worst moments. Finally, hung over from a night of heavy drinking and coming home from church of all places, she eventually relents, curses, and mutters, "All right, you can come in."

If you've heard the faint sound in the distance or seen the cat scratching outside your door, now is the time to pay attention. I'm sure it will come to you in your own way, but you need to understand something: you've been made for these times. And you're not alone. It might be your background, your experiences, your faith, even your deepest sadness that has brought you here. I promise, God is up to something in you. And it is good.

THIS IS YOUR

CHANCE

TO SAY

yes...

Part II | **THE INVITATION**

My favorite stories involve a hopeful but unequipped and unprepared protagonist who goes on to achieve their goals anyway. Despite the privileged background or technological advancements of their adversaries, the protagonist succeeds on hard work alone, driven by something deep within that can't be bought or sold.

At one point in their journey, there is a catalytic moment, a spark of inspiration that ignites an oil field of potential. The anthemic soundtrack kicks in. A high energy training montage usually follows.

I'm fascinated by that spark, the matchstick ignited in a dark room that becomes the flame for the world's most compelling stories. While the spark is exciting, we often overlook what happens before the inspiration. What does it take for the match of sulfur to glide across the striking surface of sand and powdered glass?

I believe every good spark needs an invitation, a reason to

burn in the first place. The "why" of our journey has to come before the "how."

Just as mine did for me, your invitation may start small, a whisper of an idea causing you to wonder, "It couldn't possibly be that, could it?" Your invitation may come as surprise, like an exotic postcard covered in foreign stamps, sent from an old friend across the world.

When your invitation arrives, if you're paying attention, the light in you may leap up and awake to the opportunity at hand. It is here the matches arrive, ready to ignite your invitation into a bonfire of meaning and purpose.

The following section highlights my personal inspiration and invitation—the reason I believe God made me the way he did for the challenging times we find ourselves in. You'll also learn of a powerful story from the hills of France in 1940. It's the most compelling tale I know of ordinary people who are made for these times.

Chapter 3

A MOMENT OF OBLIGATION

We are too young to realize that certain things are impossible . . . So we will do them anyway.

———

WILLIAM WILBERFORCE

It was early October, technically still fall, but the winter rains had already begun. Typical Portland. The first large drops splashed aimlessly against the fourth-floor windows of Cramer Hall at Portland State University. I was in my first semester of graduate school, staring through the window into the cloud cover of downtown Portland.

I couldn't believe just how lucky I was. Years prior, I'd continued the Zoradi legacy as the fourteenth in my family to attend

Westmont College, a spectacular liberal arts college nestled in the hills of Santa Barbara, California. I built amazing friendships, traveled in Europe for a semester during my senior year, and graduated into an ocean of first-world opportunity. My post-college years were a journey of self-discovery, leading me to Grand Rapids, Michigan, to Belfast, Northern Ireland, to Cape Town, South Africa, and then settling in Portland, Oregon.

According to Harvard and the Asian Development Bank, only 6.7 percent of the world's population holds a college degree.[1] Yet here I was, capitalizing on my privilege with a shrug of self-importance, now working through a graduate program in a field I loved in a vibrant coastal city, with a passport full of stamps and experiences. By all outward accounts, I was on track to success.

But something was off. My soul was heavy.

Months prior, while working in the sprawling townships of Cape Town's poverty-scorched underbelly, I had stumbled upon a story I couldn't put down and people I couldn't forget. When I left the South African sun for the rainy mist of the Pacific Northwest, I made a promise both to myself and to a team of high school soccer players with dreams of attending university that I would do something, anything, to stay connected and help them. The responsibility hung there like an anvil of guilt, slowing me down, keeping me awake at night.

The rain slowed as class ended and I walked through Portland's leafy park blocks with a teriyaki bowl from a local food truck. Like every good Oregonian, I had closeted my California ways and left the umbrella to gather dust in my apartment. Sitting on a park bench, thinking fondly of friends

I had met in Cape Town months before, the still, small voice of God asked the most pivotal question of my young life:

Justin. Will you deny for others what you demand for yourself?

Like the buzzing delay of antique lights switching on, the inspiration finally hit, followed by a refreshing jolt of motivation. The weight began to lift just slightly.

While I failed to realize it at the time, I was experiencing what social scientists call a "moment of obligation"—a specific time in a person's life where they feel compelled to act on a relationship, emotion, or experience. If harnessed correctly, a moment of obligation can become a person's North Star, driving them forward through the darkness of unknown terrain.[2] If powerful enough, it can reframe future experiences and commitments forever, becoming a source of lifelong meaning. While the "aha moment" is important, it's the action afterward that is truly significant.

Convicted in this moment and channeling my relationships from South Africa, I dropped a half-eaten teriyaki bento into a trash can and begin the ten-block trek to one of Portland's most famous landmarks: Powell's City of Books, spanning one full city block. Beneath the tidal wave of volumes, I acted on my obligation and purchased a book, *How to Start and Build a Nonprofit Organization.* $16.99. I placed the book inside my coat and walked back through the Pearl District toward my apartment in Chinatown. Guided by Dr. King's "fierce urgency of now," I committed on that day to doing something, anything, to give back just a sliver of the opportunities I'd been so generously afforded.

There was only one problem. I had limped through to

a C-minus in my one and only business class in college and didn't have the faintest clue about starting or growing an organization. So naive were my ambitions, I thought it timely to start a business based on the charity of others at the height of the 2008 financial crisis. I was in graduate school full time and working at a coffee shop some friends had opened in Portland's newly minted Pearl District. So, from 10:00 p.m. to the wee hours of the morning, I began researching how to start an education organization in Africa.

I was expecting the research to fuel my inspiration. It did the exact opposite.

I'd come across horrifying statistics about the HIV/AIDS infection rate in South Africa or the fact that by the time you and I finish dinner, something like 29,000 children have already died today because of entirely preventable causes.[3] Reports like this actually do the opposite of what they were intended. A harrowing statistic about infant mortality made me *less likely* to want to engage with global issues. From behind my screen they were telling me that the problems of the world are far too big for me to solve, so what is the point in trying. I was numbed.

Thankfully, the relationships with my South African friends were powerful. Anda, Michael, Ace, and Xolani kept me going. Our friendships were authentic. Tangible. Human. In that first year, I spent hundreds of dollars on Skype credit, making phone calls at 2:00 a.m., rocking an outdated call-center–style headset. After every phone call, I was reminded that no matter what the data says, my African friends weren't statistics on an Excel document or segments on a pie graph stained red. I had no idea what our little project was going to become, but I wanted my African friends to be known as more than media hype and data sets. They were people with hopes and beliefs, dreams and desires, who wanted for their families and communities the exact same things we wanted for ours. Focusing on relationships allowed me not to be impressed by the size of the challenge ahead or completely disheartened by the numbers I was seeing in reports. It was personal, and it mattered.

Calling our little movement *"These Numbers Have Faces"* fit. My then girlfriend, now wife, Trisha, coined the phrase after going over my extensive analysis of keywords and manifesto-style slogans. It was a perfect representation of our desire to prioritize people over statistics.

In those early days, running the organization from my couch, I was doggedly persistent on one key thing: I wanted to do work that matters. I was tired of watching my friends stagger home from work, ties cinched tight around their necks, caught in the endless cycle of soulless work for a mediocre salary and two weeks of vacation a year.

I've come to believe that God works by invitation. He invites us to take part in his grand redemption of the world, and in doing so, we are miraculously redeemed ourselves. His first invitation to us is the personal one, the opportunity to turn over our brokenness, to be made whole again, forgiven inside and out.

But as Shane Claiborne writes, "I came to realize that preachers were telling me to lay my life at the foot of the cross and weren't giving me anything to pick up."[4] The second invitation is our chance to pick something up, not just reveling in the beauty of being made whole. It's now about how we will reflect the light of Christ into the lives of others.

I came to understand that God's invitations arrive not by

grand choruses or trumpet blasts. His invitations rarely emerge at red carpet galas or ribbon-cutting ceremonies. Instead, they manifest themselves in stealth ways, through small, guileless interactions. Jesus rode into Jerusalem on the back of a donkey, not on a golden chariot. I've come to believe that the God of the universe prefers to initiate his people through small, simple tasks—a hidden opportunity, a spiritual head nod. A chance to say yes or no. If you say yes, the next one comes, and it's a little bit bigger. You say yes, and you trust. Then the next, then the next. When you say no, especially to the first one, it becomes just a fleeting moment, one you may never remember happening. A missed opportunity.

I've always wondered if those missed opportunities from God are stored somewhere in the spiritual realm. Perhaps in a massive, inconspicuous warehouse with forklifts and laborers. A warehouse we'll never be allowed to see because the content of the shelves would cause great sadness. It would be painful to open up a massive box with your name on it and see all the missed opportunities God had brought before you. A chance to touch a life, to care for someone else, to be cared for yourself, or maybe just to sit contently with Jesus in the passenger seat of your car, fidgeting with the radio dials.

When your invitation comes, you say yes and step out of the boat shaking, terrified. This is the only way it works. Then a little bit of confidence, a few steps forward, then more fear. Like Peter in the Sea of Galilee, it all started fine, but you're sinking now. You look up to the reassuring eyes of Christ, say yes again, and trust—a few steps more.

To this day, I don't fully know why I did it—why I said yes to a handful of South African friends and promised our relationship wouldn't end after I went home. Why I said yes to a moment of obligation on a park bench and told my family I was going to commit the next years of my life to help a few kids in South Africa go to college.

The only explanation is that God had something bigger in mind than I could ever imagine. While we started small, our little band of true believers listened intently to our African friends about what impact could be made. Together, we were inspired by the idea that nations thrive under good leadership. Whether it be in government, business, church, or in the community, ethical and moral leaders committed to their people are the ones who truly make a difference.

Through investing in future entrepreneurs, doctors, politicians, lawyers, scientists, and engineers, we began to believe young Africans could go on to solve problems and develop their own countries. With enough educated and skilled citizens, maybe one day their nations could lessen the influence of foreign aid and international organizations because they already had the ingredients for shared prosperity. Even more important was the desire to see everyone involved, me included, transformed into the people God made us to be.

I still can't wrap my head around how a few relationships with South African soccer players would grow These Numbers Have Faces into a micro-movement of global supporters walking side by side with Africa's future leaders. Or how we would expand to East Africa and go on to invest in hundreds of university students and young entrepreneurs, impacting the lives of thousands of people every year.

I never could have envisioned our graduates going on to work at some of the world's largest companies, start innovative enterprises of their own, employ their communities, and pull families out of poverty. Best of all was realizing the way my own vocation, salvation, and liberation had become beautifully bound up in the lives of our friends. As Dr. King reminds us, "We are tied together, in a single garment of destiny."[5]

It all begins with the invitation, a simple choice of yes or no to carry the thread that binds us a few inches closer to the completion of God's grand tapestry. I began to learn that my invitation wasn't an isolated incident. Rather, it was the result of millions before me who have been asked the same question in their moments of quiet reflection. "Will you deny for others what you demand for yourself?" And it was their answers, their willingness to be co-workers with God, that created the opportunities we live with today. As it will be our responses that will inspire others long after we are gone.

Chapter 4

THE CONSPIRACY
OF GOODNESS

*Do your little bit of good where you are;
it's those little bits of good put together
that overwhelm the world.*

———

DESMOND TUTU

Largely unnoticed in European history books is the tiny French village of Le Chambon. Mountainous, impoverished, and easily overlooked, the small town of Le Chambon represents a miracle of unparalleled compassion. During the four years of the German occupation of France in the 1940s, this sleepy town helped nearly five thousand Jews, most of them children, navigate through Nazi-occupied France into neutral Switzerland.

Like so many great endeavors, the story of Le Chambon began with a very small action. On a cold, dark evening in the winter of 1940, there was a knock at the door of André Trocmé, the Protestant minister of Le Chambon. Roused from his seat near the fire, he answered, and there stood a hungry, cold woman. She was a Jewish refugee fleeing the Nazis. Could she come in?

Trocmé said yes. A tiny matchstick of a word.

Little did he know, this simple act of kindness would ignite a highly organized rescue effort wherein ordinary French villagers harbored thousands of refugees in their private homes, hotels, and farms. Trocmé's response to a moment of obligation inspired his fellow villagers to enroll Jewish children in local schools, claim them as their own to government officials, and forge ration cards by candlelight to ensure the refugees were safe and fed.

When word of a Nazi raid was imminent, the residents of Le Chambon moved Jewish refugees to the countryside. One of the villagers later recalled, "As soon as the soldiers left, we would go into the forest and sing a song. When they heard that song, the Jews knew it was safe to come home."[1]

The conspiracy of goodness in Le Chambon wasn't only for the most courageous. Reports indicate that nearly every home hid Jews, not for days, but for years. So deep was their commitment that no resident of Le Chambon ever turned away, denounced, or betrayed a single Jewish refugee. Elizabeth Koenig-Kaufman was a former child refugee in Le Chambon and described her experience like this: "Nobody asked who was

Jewish and who was not. Nobody asked where you were from. Nobody asked who your father was or if you could pay. They just accepted each of us, taking us in with warmth, sheltering children, often without their parents—children who cried in the night from nightmares."[2]

Right under the nose of the Gestapo, the residents of Le Chambon, often poverty stricken themselves, protected the Jews despite risk to their own lives. In June of 1943, the German police raided a local secondary school and sent five Jewish students to Auschwitz. They also arrested their teacher, Daniel Trocmé—Pastor Trocmé's cousin—and deported him to the concentration camp, where he was killed.

Soon thereafter, Pastor Trocmé himself was identified as the leader of the operation. He was arrested and interned in a French prison camp for twenty-eight days. During his interrogation, the French government demanded he cease his illegal activities. His response was clear: "These people came here for help and for shelter. I am their shepherd. A shepherd does not forsake his flock. I do not know what a Jew is. I know only human beings."[3]

History books tell us it is great men and great armies who make history. Compared to the mighty military campaigns of World War II, the story of Le Chambon is a small one. The worth of moral action is often measured by the number of people it impacts, so ordinary individuals affecting the lives of a few are easily overlooked. With nearly 70 million lives lost in World War II, a few French eccentrics in Le Chambon did virtually nothing to stop Hitler's war machine and death camps. Their mountainous village was an irrelevant drop in the bottomless ocean of war.

But in the secret rooms and converted attic spaces of Le

Chambon, the actions of a Protestant minister and a few hundred allies were far from insignificant. They believed God acts in stealthy ways, under the radar, and so should they. They believed Christian compassion was tangible, a light of goodness filtering under door frames, shining in dark corners, and chasing out shadows. They believed each individual life saved was one step closer to the end of the war. Despite any criticism of their tireless work in this century or the last, the Chambonnais remind us, "Real people with their own proper names saved real human beings in that village. And these precious few people count."[4]

The actions in Le Chambon were carried out not by City Hall or the Red Cross but by individual citizens in the privacy of their homes, led by both men and women alike. In their daily decisions of courage, mostly at their kitchen tables and in small groups, the Chambonnais shouldered the crushing need of the world, and they did so gladly. André Trocmé's wife, Magda, even considered their actions a "hobby" for her and her friends, as they skillfully smuggled Jews into neutral Switzerland through a highly organized underground network. They were ordinary citizens motivated by the preciousness of each human life, acting in the moment for the right purpose.

André and Magda Trocmé would later reflect on their lives and remember 1934 to 1944 in Le Chambon as their happiest years. It is when they believe they did their most important work. In the 1970s, an American named Philip Hallie spent a few months in Le Chambon, conducting research for a book he would later write, called *Lest Innocent Blood Be Shed*, which chronicled the story of the heroic Chambonnais.

In almost every interview Hallie had with the Chambonnais, they were put off by the moral complexity of his questioning and confused as to why he was exploring this topic at all. Hallie writes that there came a moment when nearly every interviewee would pull back and look firmly into his eyes. One after another, they responded with, "How can you call us 'good'? We were doing what had to be done. Who else could help them? You must understand that it was the most natural thing in the world to help these people."[5]

Their "good" deeds were nothing more than an instinct, a natural reflex in the body of Christ. For the villagers of Le Chambon, the question that arose from Nazism wasn't how could God allow such evil to occur, but how God works through ordinary people to combat such evil. Rather than over-theologizing and overanalyzing, the Chambonnais jumped in headfirst. There wasn't time to attend a conference on orchestrating a social movement or wait for a diploma to hang on an office wall. Guided by a belief in humanity and true feelings of empathy, they met in their one-room church, trained themselves, and changed the world.

The astounding compassion of these French commoners has humbled me greatly. Yet, as modern people looking back on history, we have the tendency to romanticize its dissidents into superhuman saints, immortalized in stained glass. The courage of the Chambonnais seems almost *Marvel-comic* worthy, existing in a time and place outside the human experience. But we can't forget that the Chambonnais were farmers, builders, stay-at-home moms, and schoolteachers. Being ordinary is what made them powerful.

Just like you and me, the Chambonnais were made for their time in history. As I've reflected deeply on what it means to be made for these times and do work that matters, one thing has become clear: this is as much about our own personal and spiritual development as it is anything else. My quest for meaning happened to begin across the world, but the principles in this book are for all types of people, no matter where you live or what you do. A life of purpose isn't about what you're doing; it's about who you are becoming. As David Brooks writes, "Social transformation flows from personal transformation. You change the world when you hold up a new and more attractive way to live."[6]

———

The remainder of the book is broken into four sections, *"The Grit," "The Companions," "The Momentum,"* and *"The Commissioning."* Operating like a road map for your journey, over the next microchapters we'll develop the skills we need to fend off our demons. We'll cultivate our character, rally others around us, and find the balance necessary for a lifetime of impact. We'll commit to doing incomplete work, trust others to pick up where we leave off, and humbly pursue spiritual development as the foundation for it all.

As you read this book, I hope you'll see that my goal isn't to be the hero of this story. Rather, it is to operate as your guide as you navigate what it means to be made for these times. If you've found yourself in the pursuit of purpose or in the early stages of your noble quest, pay attention to what's coming next. Whether it's inside the walls of your home, working in your community, or jetsetting across the world, the following topics, stories, and lessons are critical to thriving in a life that matters. The heroes of our history were ordinary, just like you and me. They were made for these times. And here's the real kicker: you're up next.

Now the

REAL WORK

begins . . .

Part III | THE GRIT

Maybe you're like me. You've walked home on a warm summer night or have been driving in your car when the perfect song comes on. For a brief moment you've sensed the person you were born to be.

Perhaps you've already been invited into the life you most want to live. You've had a compelling moment of obligation and can faintly see the road ahead.

But for many of us, as soon as we begin the first steps down our path of purpose, toward the thing we know we are made for, we find it's booby trapped like the Temple of Doom. As we lose our footing down the slippery slope and the spikes shoot from the walls, we realize it is a million times easier to retreat than go forward.

Terrified and unprepared, we apologize to ourselves for putting our one precious life in harm's way.

People who are made for these times are able to walk through the forests of fear. They do it every day. They know who they are and what they are made for, and they refuse to settle for anything less.

Even more remarkable, they have the amazing ability to take what they believe and turn it into what they do. They make the impractical practical, the unrealistic a reality.

The following chapters chronicle the personal trials we will inevitably battle on our quest for meaning. We'll dig deep to find our grit, name the resistance we face, and pursue—as Eugene Peterson famously recommends—a long obedience in the same direction.

Chapter 5

SANDPAPER

Simple unvarying constancy and long perseverance is much more impressive than any miracle.

———

ST. MARTIN DE PORRES

Each summer, about twelve hundred highly motivated young people arrive at the United States Military Academy at West Point. With an acceptance rate of only ten percent, these new recruits represent the best of the best. But before any of them sees a classroom, they endure seven grueling weeks of Cadet Basic Training. As Daniel Pink describes in his ground-breaking book on human motivation, by the time the summer ends, sixty of the 1200 will have already dropped out.

A group of researchers wanted to understand why some students survived basic training and continued their military careers while others barely made it out of the gate. Pink asks, "Was it physical strength and athleticism? Intellect? Leadership ability? Well-roundedness?"[1]

Turns out, it was none of the above. Researchers found the best predictor of success was the cadets' scores on a "noncognitive, nonphysical trait known as 'grit.'"

In her excellent book and TED Talk on this research, Angela Duckworth describes grit as "perseverance and passion for long term goals. Grit is having stamina. Grit is sticking with what is in front of you, day in and day out. Not just for the week, not just for the month, but for years."[2]

Grit is that special force that gets you down in the dirt. Grit is toil. Grit is the slow burn over time that nearly kills you, and yet it's the best indicator for success. So much so that researchers found in every field, grit was just as important as talent. For college students, it was grittiness rather than IQ or standardized test scores that was the most accurate predictor of college grades. Because grit is such a powerful indicator for success, it becomes the lifeblood of some of the world's greatest stories. Grit is *Rocky Balboa*, the *Mighty Ducks*, and J. K. Rowling when *Harry Potter* was rejected by publishers twelve times.

I'm a massive soccer fan. For many Americans, soccer is an acquired taste, like beer or coffee—or baseball. While it can be thrilling and dramatic, there are times when—and I hate to admit it—it can be kind of boring. The thing I've learned as I've begun to study the game is a key difference between good teams and great teams. Good teams win when they play well. Great teams "grind out wins" when they're playing poorly. It's not pretty, and there are few fireworks. But they defend well, keep the ball, don't stretch themselves too thin, and toil their way to a 1–0 or 2–1 victory. This is the short-term sports version of grit. It's not inspiring, but it works.

Here's a fitting metaphor: sandpaper is measured in the size of its grit. Tiny bumps on a piece of paper grind down larger items over time, making them smooth and manageable. While talent is obviously helpful, grit is the X factor to long-term success. If I've learned anything from people who are made for these times, it's that they embody grit to the nth degree. My one piece of advice is this: if you don't have grit, you need to find it. If you already have it, don't waste it on something insignificant.

Despite the advancements in neuroscience, the measurement of human grit is remarkably hard to quantify. Some say you have to experience great adversity to get it. Others just seem to be born with it. At this point in time, there is no formula for how to harness and cultivate grit. It can't be synthesized into pill form or purchased from a health food store. I believe the science comes up short on grit because its manifestation within us is extraordinarily personal and subjective. Grit is something deep within you; it's the soul of your purpose only you can discover how to access.

However, one tool I've used to develop my own grit is learning as much as possible about the gritty experiences of others. When we uncover real-life stories of grit in action, they can act as the inspiration we need to harness it ourselves. This means we should always be on the lookout for stories of people triumphing in the face of adversity. I believe the more we surround ourselves with the inspiration of others, the more we'll internalize the possibility of doing it in our own lives.

Chapter 6

HOPE STARTS HERE

*Sometimes courage is the quiet voice
at the end of the day saying, "I will try
again tomorrow."*

―――――

MARY ANNE RADMACHE

The tarped ceilings are branded in big blue letters: UNHCR. It's a daily reminder that the Gihembe Refugee Camp is meant to be temporary. A roof made of white plastic sheeting hardly keeps out the cold, and when it rains, it beats down like rapid-fire percussion. For more than twenty years, fifteen thousand Congolese refugees have been living in a camp constructed and managed by the United Nations High Commission for Refugees (UNHCR). Gihembe sits atop a muddy hill an hour outside of the capital city of Kigali, Rwanda. There is one tiny school, few businesses, and little civic authority. Mud-walled huts offer no electricity or basic comforts much of the world takes for granted. Families huddle side by side on cheap mats, spooning each other to maximize the body-to-mat ratio.

The United Nations provides each refugee $0.24 a day, sent via mobile money transfer to a single cell phone per family. Too desperate to marvel at the innovative genius of mobile currency, the daily allotment provides one meal a day, mainly of beans and rice, and a potato if you're lucky. In Gihembe there is nothing to do except to sit. For more than twenty years, people have been sitting.

Without stimulation, the human brain slowly begins to shut down. Synapses fail to fire, kinetic energy begins to fade. The first things to go are attributes like creativity, drive, and passion. Like dew, they evaporate into the air, only to return as rain clouds of cynicism stewing overhead. Yet the residents of Gihembe will gladly take a prison with no walls over what could have been. In 1996, they narrowly escaped as the genocide in Rwanda spilled into the Eastern Congo. They ran for their lives and hid in bug-infested jungles, children in tow, as armed militias hunted them down with machetes and guns. The refugees of Gihembe bear the physical and emotional scars of genocide. I've been in a lot of hard places, but I'd never seen anything like this.

Robert and Elizabeth Bjork are psychologists at UCLA who penned the notion of "desirable difficulties." The Bjorks were interested in shaking up the education theory that when learning is made easiest, performance naturally improves. Instead they theorized that in special cases, learning can greatly improve when the environment is made infinitely harder. They believed that in certain instances, when the forces of difficulty are so extreme, a select group of highly intelligent individuals actually perceive the challenge as *desirable* and will rise up to fight. Such is the case in Gihembe. The challenges of the refugee camp are so extreme, the poverty so real, that while most are knocked down by injustice, there are cases where special people find the motivation to move mountains.

One of those mountain movers is a young man named Jean Paul. His family fled the Congo when he was three, and he carries no memories of his homeland. The oldest son in a family of ten, Jean Paul was always fascinated by science and electricity. Rigging up mini lights from discarded batteries, he brought tiny amounts of electricity into their mud hut to the awe of his neighbors. It was in a tiny primary school in Gihembe that Jean Paul began his education. His grades in science and math caught the attention of secondary schools outside the camp, and he was one of the privileged few who received a scholarship to a nearby private high school.

As a Congolese refugee, he was always an outsider to his Rwandan peers, who, while poor themselves, could never comprehend life in a refugee camp. It's impossible to draw the line on when and where the theory of desirable difficulties begins and ends, but in the case of Jean Paul, the stars aligned perfectly. Desperately poor at home and marginalized at school, he fought for every shred of information, every kernel of knowledge. When the Rwandan High School National Exam rolled around, to the surprise of everyone, he received a perfect score and was ranked the number-two high school student in the entire country.

Every year, the top thirty Rwandan students are vetted to receive the Rwandan Presidential Scholarship, a full scholarship provided by the government to a prestigious American university. After an intensive round of interviews and tests, the top seventeen are offered the scholarship personally by Rwandan President Paul Kagame. With his stellar test scores, Jean Paul qualified for the first round of consideration.

On the day he heard he'd been selected, he burst through the flimsy door of his mud-walled hut. His family members gathered as he exclaimed, "I am one of the top thirty! I might be going to America!" Screams burst forth as the family hugged and cried together. This was the opportunity they had been waiting for. After running for their lives during the genocide and living over twenty years isolated in a refugee camp, here was their chance to rewrite the family story.

Eric, one of Jean Paul's friends from Gihembe, had also been selected as one of the thirty Presidential Scholarship candidates. Together they'd be heading to the capital city for a meeting at the Department of Education. The day finally came. They boarded a bus to Kigali, waved goodbye to their families, and sped off toward the city, dreaming of a far-off land called America.

Arriving at the Ministry of Education in mismatched suits borrowed from friends and neighbors, Jean Paul and Eric turned their heads upward, marveling at the tall buildings and traffic-jammed roundabouts. Shaking with excitement, they entered a room with twenty-eight other students to begin the full day of testing. Jean Paul blew through the academic portion of the test, especially the math section. His in-person interviews went just as well. Possessed with optimism, he was candid, engaging, and funny. The administrator smiled and handed him a packet with his final score, already tallied. It read 77/80, a near-perfect score. There was nothing stopping him now.

The administrator led him down a long hallway to sign some final paperwork. Buzzing with elation, he entered a room with a representative of the president. Congratulating him on his academic ability and a top score on the president's exam, as a matter of formality the representative asked to see Jean Paul's national identification card to begin the paperwork. Stunned, Jean Paul explained that he was a refugee from the Gihembe camp outside Kigali, and he didn't have a Rwandan identity card.

"You are Congolese?" she inquired.

"Yes," he replied.

"Then, I'm very sorry, the Presidential Scholarship is only for citizens of Rwanda."

Taken aback, he stammered, "Yes, but I've been living in Rwanda nearly my entire life. I attended Rwandan schools. We were driven out of the Congo by the militias, the ones your government stopped from killing us." He pleaded, "We are Tutsi, just like his Excellency, President Kagame."

"I'm very sorry," the administrator replied. "Without Rwandan national identification documents, we cannot offer you the scholarship."

"Can I perhaps receive support to attend university here in Rwanda? My family is very poor, and we cannot afford it. That has to be a much more affordable option than going to America. Can President Kagame provide us with that?"

"I'm sorry again," she replied. "As a Congolese refugee,

the government of Rwanda cannot offer you any assistance for higher education. You will have to find another way."

Devastation.

With his head in his hands, Jean Paul slumped on a bench outside the Department of Education. There was no hope now. His friend Eric joined him. He'd received a 75/80, placing him in the top seventeen as well. But like Jean Paul, his refugee status disqualified him.

Jean Paul's story is not an isolated incident. There are millions of students from all over Africa who are incredible scholars with no future of a university education. It's infinitely harder for refugees who don't possess the correct documentation in the countries where they reside. The tragedy here is systemic, pigeonholing the next generation of aspiring students into a life without options. If young people see top students like Jean Paul back in the refugee camp, splitting firewood for a living, what's the point of working hard in school at all? Why dream any bigger if the future is just a life inside the camp anyway?

It was the spring of 2013 when These Numbers Have Faces first heard the story of the Gihembe camp and students like Jean Paul. At first we couldn't believe the academic scores we were seeing. How could students from a refugee camp, students who began their education on dirt floors with tarped ceilings, possibly get perfect scores on the national exams and rank nationally against the sons and daughters of diplomats and parliamentarians? The world simply doesn't work this way.

Scovia, our program director in Rwanda, pulled some strings with higher-ups at the United Nations, and we were granted clearance to travel to Gihembe ourselves. Exiting the van, it was clear that this was a place that has had very few visitors. Little kids immediately began screaming "Mzungu! Mzungu!" ("white person") and then would duck into doorways, embarrassed. We traversed through the camp, meeting people, hearing stories, and taking in the savagery of Gihembe. Our team exchanged worried glances, communicating without words and asking each other, "How can people live like this?" But there was something different as well. Gihembe also represented a "thin place," a term coined by Celtic monks on the windswept islands of Scotland, where the veil between heaven and earth felt closer than usual. There was desperation, but something beautiful was rumbling.

The heartbeat of our visit was the Hope School. Armed with homemade shovels and the human power of determined hands, Hope School was constructed by high school students in 2008. The UN had built a primary school years earlier, but there were no resources for older students. With their education ending at ninth grade, they were doomed—the cycle of poverty spinning at record speeds. The UN told them point blank, "If you want a school, you will have to build it yourselves." With mud, bricks, and sticks, students toiled for an entire summer until four walls, a tarped roof, and a door were raised. They found volunteer teachers, photocopied chapters of textbooks, and began to teach themselves. A single math book was smuggled in from a school outside the camp, its tattered pages enriching the minds of two hundred students at a time. As we walked into Hope School on that fateful day, we saw math equations covering a single chalkboard and a slender young man with a toothy grin, his hands covered in chalk. He introduced himself.

"My name is Jean Paul, welcome to Hope School."

After losing the Presidential Scholarship, there was nothing left to do but teach at the Hope School, believing that one day, one of his pupils would make it further than he could. The rain poured down as our team huddled together in the school doorway, debating about what to do. Jean Paul's lectures carried like a soundtrack in the background. The headmaster of Hope School knew about our current work with university students in Kigali and had smartly mobilized many of the top Gihembe students to meet us.

We aren't an organization with millions of dollars at our disposal. Every student we select goes through a rigorous application process, and at that time we didn't have the funds to add any more students. But the story of Gihembe was simply too big to pass up. Just in case, we had brought stacks of These Numbers Have Faces university application forms and thought we might as well start handing them out. Squatting on the dirt floor with the applications on their knees, we watched an entire room of students writing furiously with dull pencils.

We were set to fly out from Rwanda the next day, so we left Gihembe early and our program director, Scovia, promised to come back the next day to gather the applications. On the ride home, our team decided we would select twelve of the top students from Gihembe that had been shut out by the Rwandan government. We didn't have the money yet, but we promised we would find it. Our Rwandan staff spent the next few weeks poring over applications and conducting interviews in Gihembe. They settled on the top candidates, and Scovia excitedly jumped on the phone to break the news to the lucky students.

Eric, a tall kid, was sitting in the darkness of his family

home when he got the call. He says he screamed and jumped up, hitting his head on the tarped ceiling and separating a wooden beam that would have to be fixed later. Soon Dogon, Yvonne, Lenny, Jeannine, Hyranzi, Promise, Claude, Gerald, Alice, and Modest all got phone calls. Of course, we could never forget Jean Paul. He got one too.

After the calls went out, the headmaster at Hope School called Scovia back.

"The whole camp is celebrating," the headmaster said with joy in his voice. "People are overjoyed because their top twelve students are going to university."

It was in that moment that God breathed life into our little movement. We were truly on to something. Back in Portland, I began sharing the story of Gihembe. Miraculously, a generous foundation stepped up and gave us funds to pay the first semester of tuition, room, and board for the Gihembe scholars. A few weeks later, twelve Gihembe students were on the bus to Kigali, their simple possessions bound together in small plastic bags, to join our existing Rwanda program.

Now years later, hundreds of refugees apply to join These Numbers Have Faces each year, and nearly 40 percent of our East African programs benefit refugee students. We've expanded to other refugee camps around the region, and our scholars have gone on to graduate, secure impressive jobs, start entrepreneurial ventures of their own, win awards, and travel the world.

While this was not an explicit part of our organization's vision, Jean Paul got his shot at America after all when his whole family was resettled to the United States by the United Nations to Oregon, of all places. He secured a full scholarship to finish his engineering studies at the prestigious University of Portland, achieved straight A's throughout, and now works at Intel as a software engineer.

When you talk to Jean Paul, he often also reflects on the difficulty of his circumstances and how they shaped him into the person he is today. Growing up in a refugee camp, struggling to eat every day, losing out on the scholarship to America, volunteering at Hope School, and then finally getting his chance to achieve his dreams, he often jokes about how any challenge he faces now is simple compared to what he's already been through.

The grit he developed in the refugee camp embodies the Bjorks' theory of "desirable difficulties." The learning environment was so extreme that the desire to fight back has made Jean Paul and others nearly impenetrable to challenging circumstances thereafter. As the monastics say, "The highest form of sanctity is to live in hell and not lose hope."[1]

Chapter 7

THE RESISTANCE

*It's better to be in the arena, getting
stomped by the bull, than to be up in the
stands or out in the parking lot.*

STEVEN PRESSFIELD

I'm jolted awake at 3:00 a.m., soaked in sweat. It happens to be August, but the seasons don't matter. This happens all times of the year. The ceiling fan above is whirring, the windows are open. Portland's dry heat lays heavy in my upstairs bedroom. As soon as I'm conscious, the first waves of fear and dread start to pour over me. I try to shut it down, distancing my mind from the flash, throwing any thought on top of it to bury the impact. A relaxing holiday at the beach, soccer lineups of my favorite teams, house projects I want to work on. But it's too late. My spiraling mind blasts through my defenses and unearths the mountain of work to do, deadlines to hit, people to please, promises to fulfill, and all of it resting . . . on . . . me.

This is all too familiar now. I know exactly what it is: The Resistance.

Our first office for These Numbers Have Faces was basically a glorified storage unit in a run-down building against the south side of Portland's iconic Burnside Bridge—a structure as famous for what lies beneath it as on top. Burnside Avenue cuts the city in half, the bridge a six-lane link between the east and west and a roof for the seedy underbelly of the iconic Burnside Skatepark.

I had dragged myself to the office but barely made it out of the parking lot. Defeated, I sat under the Burnside Bridge, the roar of trucks above and skateboard wheels grinding their way to punk stardom in the skatepark below. I was smoking a cigarette I'd bummed from some other parking lot loser. Pathetic.

We'd launched a fundraising campaign a few days earlier to a lukewarm response. The staff had gone home, our air conditioning was broken, and the office was hot, sluggish, and uninviting. I felt tired. Overwhelmed by the task and sinking in the shallow depth of what we were trying to accomplish thousands of miles away, for the thousandth time I heard: *Who do you think you are, trying to help people across the world? No one cares. You're not good enough. You never will be. Quit now and get a real job.*

If you haven't read Steven Pressfield's groundbreaking books *The War of Art* and *Do the Work*, you may want to put this down and pick up one of those instead. The Pressfield book you've probably heard of is *The Legend of Bagger Vance*, which was adapted into a movie starring Will Smith as a golf caddy during the Great Depression.

Pressfield has given a name to one of the greatest adversaries we'll ever fight: *The Resistance*. I believe in The Resistance. You should too. If you haven't heard of it before, here's what you need to know.

There is an enemy. It is an active and intelligent force whose only mission is to destroy you. Pressfield writes how The Resistance cannot be seen, touched, heard, or smelled. But it can be felt. It is a cunning adversary with no conscience that will stop at nothing to keep you from becoming the person you were made to be.

The Resistance is a soul crusher, a dream dasher, a seductive whisperer hell-bent on distracting and double-crossing people like you and me. You may not have known its name, but if you're a human being and have attempted anything noble, entrepreneurial, creative, weight-loss inducing, or self-enhancing, you've been in the ring with The Resistance whether you've known it or not.

Like Andrew Garfield on the River Thames, The Resistance is your own sinister thoughts declaring you aren't good enough and never will be. It is the fire alarm in your head pleading with you to give up when the vice starts to tighten. The Resistance is the words of your friends from high school who pressure you to revert back to the person you were in a former life. It's also the sweet tone of your well-meaning family who would rather you stay safe and just "be happy."

The simple fact that you've picked up this book has alerted The Resistance to your quest. It smells blood in the water. The

Resistance will start passively at first, mainly with requests of procrastination, aiming to calmly convince you to waste your time and discard your gifts. It hopes you'll begin to believe on your own that you have nothing to offer this world.

But when you resist its siren song, that's when the tension starts to escalate. And on the day when a breakthrough is imminent, when you begin truly acting like you're made for these times, trust me, the flaming arrows will start to rain down. It is in these moments that you'll be pinned to your bed in agony, aimlessly succumbing to bad habits, and inches away from throwing in the towel on whatever dream you had the day before.

As a person of faith, The Resistance is just another word for the dark forces in the world that I believe are all too real. C. S. Lewis personifies these in the *Screwtape Letters* as Satan's minions, whose mission is to trip us up, cause chaos, and disconnect us from God.

Perhaps the Devil's genius isn't that he turns people into mini-evil versions of himself but rather gets them so preoccupied with their own inner monologue that they never break out of being insecure, mediocre, small, and soft.

To declare yourself made for these times, you must defeat The Resistance. And it's going to suck. The first step is recognizing its existence. There is immense power in naming your enemy for what it is.

The next step is turning pro. Turning pro isn't about getting some degree to hang on your wall. Turning pro is an ideal, a belief system, a personal mantra declaring you won't give into the hissing lies of The Resistance. Turning pro is a mindset alteration. It's the mental switch that defaults to fighting back. As Pressfield notes, "Resistance hates it when we turn pro."[1]

I write this as much for me as I do for you. There are a number of ways to turn pro, but these are the three that have impacted me the most.

1. Don't Overidentify with Your Work

Overidentifying with our work is one of the most powerful strategies of The Resistance. To this day I can't help but allow my identity to be shaped by the work I do or the expression of the beliefs I hold. When we overidentify with our work, the success or failure of our career or calling seeps into our own self-worth. We begin to see who we are through the lens of success in the marketplace or through the perceptions of others. I can't begin to describe just how dangerous this is. Even if our work is inspired by God, there is always danger in choosing to serve "God's work" rather than God himself. The work becomes a replacement and ultimately an idol.

Growing up, soccer was my entire life. I'd train every day with competitive teams and travel to weekend tournaments all over California. Before the invention of the internet, I would stay up until 2:00 a.m. to catch English Premier League highlights as it was impossible to find them anywhere else. After playing in front of college coaches and going through the recruiting process, I finally fulfilled my dream to play soccer at Westmont College. Unfortunately, I just wasn't good enough. I was unable to make the leap to that next level and quit after my freshman year. I'll never forget crying as I walked back to my dorm after leaving the coach's office for the last time. I kept thinking, *Without soccer, who am I? What am I?* My identity had become so wrapped up in a sport I could no longer play competitively, I had lost who I actually was.

This pattern of identity infatuation continued. My "punk phase" stretched through the rest of college and into my mid-twenties. Dyed hair and mosh pits, aggression and anarchy: a rebellion-fueled search for a new identity. That was followed by a journey into global humanitarian work, from Belfast to Cape Town, Portland to Kigali. For more than a decade, These Numbers Have Faces became my life. Slowly but surely, I built my personal identity on the success or failure of an organization that I may have started but will surely grow beyond me.

The Resistance loves those who overidentify with their work. A bad performance review, a failed startup, one mean boss, and our entire identity is on the rocks. Amateurs define themselves by their job descriptions. This is the surest way to never turning pro. Pressfield reminds us, "The amateur will never reach her goals because she's over-invested in her success and over-terrified of failure. The amateur takes her work so seriously that it paralyzes her."[2]

In the moments I've found myself paralyzed by my own identity, I'm fortunate to have a wife like the brilliant Trisha Zoradi. She said the most important thing anyone has ever said to me while I lay in our upstairs bedroom in agony, choked out by The Resistance, overidentified with my work, and convinced that my success as a person hinged on the success of my organization. Trisha rubbed my head and whispered, "You know, I'd love you the same if you made sandwiches at Subway."

That right there is unconditional love. Even if I made sandwiches for a living, she loves me not for what I do but for who I am. While this is an expression of true love from my wife, we know God's love is even deeper and more unconditional.

As Timothy Keller reminds us, "The world says you are loved because of what you do. Jesus says you can now do all things because you are loved."[3]

It's so easy to forget just how deeply loved we really are, not for our job title or how hard we work, but simply for being who we really are. In Christ, our identity is secure, no matter what. It's in this surrender of our identity that the fog of The Resistance dissipates, slinking away to regroup and come back at us tomorrow.

2. Learn to Live and Work in the Midst of Fear

On the days when The Resistance has its slimy hands around my throat, I have a few special spots I like to go in Portland to fight back. One is in Forest Park, another overlooking the docks in North Portland. They are places of calm amid the bustle of the city.

Some people say God talks to them at length. Full paragraphs and jokes and all. For me, God has been more of a broken record lately. When the world feels like it's crashing down, all I hear are the same two lines:

1. It's okay to be scared.
2. Rest in me.

I hate when I'm in the middle of it, but fear is actually good. The more you love something, the more you'll fear it, because you know it can hurt you. If you lose the fear, you lose the love. Pressfield says fear is an ally and an indicator of what you have to keep doing in life.

Self-doubt can be an ally. This is because it serves as an indicator of aspiration. It reflects love, love of something we dream of doing, and desire, desire to do it. If you find yourself asking yourself, "Am I really a writer? Am I really an artist?" chances are you are. The counterfeit innovator is wildly self-confident. The real one is scared to death.[4]

When angels appear to humans in the Bible, the first words out of their mouths are often, "Do not be afraid." They knew we'd be petrified. When I talk with fellow Christians about the nature of fear, I often hear that we should never be afraid because Christ comes to liberate us from fear. I think he does, but I also believe fear is an important indicator for what we have to keep striving after in life.

So often our future is a fog. I know mine is. My own quest to do work that matters, a fledgling writing career, my role as a husband and father—it's all steeped in mystery so thick and so dark I could choke on it. I know great things lie ahead, but at the moment, I can only see a few feet in front of me. Despite the darkness, I believe this fog is telling me something. It's telling me I'm exactly where I'm meant to be.

In times of fog, the lantern is the tool of God: a tiny light illuminating only a few steps at a time. In times of darkness, we cling to the lantern. One step and then the next. We trust the light to do its job and solidify our shaky steps. In the darkness I find myself praying for it all to be revealed. If only I could have the full vision now and see the final chapter at this moment instead of the next.

But total light would ruin the vision. It would spoil the skills and ideas meant to be honed, the relationships meant to be built, the conflict we're meant to endure. If the house lights are flipped on, illuminating the entire journey, there is no need for the lantern.

The lantern is the life force. It's our intimate connection to the Creator, the physical manifestation of God at our fingertips. Life is hard. The road is long and narrow. The workers are few. We may see more fog than light for years at a time.

But the fog is the entire point. It represents our need for the light and the confirmation of our calling. A life without fog is a life of complacency and boredom. It's like reading the last page of the novel and skipping the conflict, climax, and resolution. Our pursuit for meaning and purpose is rarely if ever written plainly on the wall. In times like these, we cling to the lantern of light.

While it is uncomfortable in the fog, we should revel in the fear we are facing, reminding ourselves it's a natural emotion and a valuable tool. But in the midst of fear, we must have confidence in God's stability and providence for us. When I'm overwhelmed by worry, fear, dread, or regret, I rush back to the foundations of my faith and these three principles from Sarah Collins:[5]

1. Our future is uncertain. This is how it is meant to be. You're not supposed to see the whole story.
2. Secret things belong to the Lord, and future things are secret things.
3. Our worry is an act of rebellion. It doubts God's promises to care for us.

In my top office drawer I have a green folder that holds some of my most prized documents. They aren't awards, certificates, or photographs; they are clippings of verses, prayers, and quotations. I've got some by Henri Nouwen, a hearty dose of Dr. King's, some from C. S. Lewis, and a pinch of Thomas Merton. These brief reflections, handwritten or printed from my office computer, act as anchors of hope in times of uncertainty. Over the last few months, my little folder has grown and grown.

The repetition of opening this folder every morning to read and reread its contents has saved me in times of anxiety. I set aside twenty minutes a day and let these familiar words pour over me. The same words from the same place, over and over. This repetition, this act of obedience, has become the foundation of my day. Miraculously, it has brought peace.

It's not uncommon to keep a first aid kit in your car or a few gallons of water in your basement for an emergency. We should follow the same guidelines for our souls. In your times of mental clarity and hopefulness, place the quotes, phrases, verses, prayers, and letters of encouragement you know you will need in times of disbelief and despair.

3. Stay Stupid

The world's first supercomputers took up entire rooms, but they held less memory than the flash drive you get for free at a university career day. Nowadays, we have access to endless information, with the machines in our pockets able to access billions of websites in seconds. But too much information can bury us under mountains of sources. For every issue there is always a competing view and a reason to go forward, stay in neutral, or put it in reverse. The Resistance wants us to overdose on information, to overthink, over-research, and overprepare. Sometimes you have to stay stupid: to think less and act first.

People who live out the fact that they are made for these times are stupid. I mean that in a good way. They don't listen to conventional wisdom. They may have no idea what they are getting themselves into or how hard the path is, but they are bold enough to try and pull it off anyway. The Wright brothers were stupid. Amelia Earhart was stupid. I started These Numbers Have Faces from my couch as the economy imploded in 2008. I had dozens of very smart people tell me I should hold off on becoming a social entrepreneur until the economy rebounded. I didn't listen because my passion outweighed the logical risk. I was stupid, and it was the best decision I ever made.

You know Martin Luther King Jr.'s "I Have a Dream" speech. But I'll bet, like me, you didn't know the full story. Gary Younge, a writer for *The Guardian*, tells it this way.[6]

> The night before the March on Washington, on August 28, 1963, Martin Luther King asked his aides for advice about the next day's speech. "Don't use the lines about 'I have a dream,' his chief adviser Wyatt Walker told him. 'It's trite, it's cliché. You've used it too many times already.'"

King had indeed used the phrase several times before, at a fundraiser in Chicago and a few months before at a rally in Detroit. But this speech at the March on Washington had to be different. King was now a national figure. Television networks would be covering the event, and buses from all over the country would be bringing people in. Organizers were expecting crowds in the hundreds of thousands. This speech would be King's official introduction to the nation.

King went to sleep at about 4:00 a.m. the night before and

gave the final text of his speech to his aides to print and distribute. The "I Have a Dream" section was not in it.

As the event began the next day, King was sixteenth in line to speak. Before him was the national anthem, an invocation, a prayer, a tribute to women, two sets of gospel songs, and then nine other speakers. By the time King approached the lecture, it was a humid 87 degrees with the noon sun scorching overhead. The crowd was hot and lethargic.

With the affirming gaze of the Lincoln Memorial behind him, King settled behind the podium and started slowly, sticking close to the prepared text. Rigid and overprepared, it seemed that he, too, could sense that it wasn't enough.

Then, from behind him on the stage, King's favorite gospel singer Mahalia Jackson cried out, "Tell 'em about the dream, Martin!" Nonplussed, King kept on with his prepared remarks. Jackson shouted again, "Tell 'em about the dream!"

This time he listened. King shuffled his notes and set the prepared text to his left, out of eyesight. It was happening. His aide and personal friend Clarence Jones recounted, "When he was reading from his text, he stood like a lecturer. But from the moment he set that text aside, he took on the stance of a Baptist preacher." Jones turned to the person standing next to him and said, "Those people don't know it, but they're about to go to church."

King bellowed,

So even though we face the difficulties of today and tomorrow, I still have a dream. It is a dream deeply rooted in the American dream. I have a dream that one day this nation will rise up and live out the true meaning of its creed . . . I have a dream that one day on the red hills of Georgia the sons of former slaves and the sons of former slave owners will be able to sit down together at the table of brotherhood . . . I have a dream that my four little children will one day live in a nation where they will not be judged by the color of their skin but by the content of their character.

Meanwhile, his chief aide Wyatt Walker cursed under his breath, shaking his head as he muttered, "He's using the dream."

Today, we all know the result of King's dream. That famous line and what spontaneously came after would forever forge King into the history books. On that warm August day in 1963, in the most important speech of his life, King dismissed his notes and went rogue in front of 250,000 people. I mean this in the most admirable way possible: Martin Luther King Jr. stayed stupid on that day. He acted out of his primal self, his most natural place. He bared his soul as a Baptist minister instead of a prepared politician. The Resistance told him to stick to the script. King didn't, and nothing will ever be the same.

———

The world needs you. Yes, you. Just like King, if you're going to become the person God created you to be, the first mountain you'll face is The Resistance telling you otherwise. But today is the day you'll fight back. Today is the day you won't overidentify; you'll own your fear, stay stupid, and move one step closer to turning pro.

I'm reminded of the impactful words of Gary Haugen from

the International Justice Mission, "When the calling of God is scary, we lead by remembering that Jesus did not come to make us safe; He came to make us brave."[7]

Depending on your theology, there are a handful of reasons Jesus came to earth centuries ago. Some say he came only to die: thirty-three sacrificial years to forgive the sins of the world and redeem humanity. Others suggest he also came for social revolution: to champion the kingdom of God, turn the system on its head, and expose the hypocrisy of the religious and political elite. I tend to accept all of the theories, believing the more Jesus the better. But I also believe, as Gary Haugen does, that Jesus came to make us brave.

You'll have to face The Resistance eventually. It's inevitable. There is no workaround, and avoiding the confrontation means you've already given in. But this isn't a battle we fight alone. The tighter we're linked to Christ, the braver we become: like Moses, inspired by God to speak in front of Pharaoh, or Esther, proudly proclaiming her faith to save her people. The ultimate tool in defeating the enemy is his power flowing through you. This is where the darkness dissipates, The Resistance fades, and the light of hope shines through.

Chapter 8

PEAK WHEN YOU'RE SIXTY

*Courage isn't always a lion's roar—it's also
the silence of an ant working persistently,
patiently and never giving up.*

———

AFRICAN PROVERB

I'll never forget the day I came across the fascinating story of Nobel Prize–winning physicist Peter Higgs. Nearly five decades ago, a young Peter Higgs theorized that there was a particle that acts as the building block of the universe. He believed that a subatomic particle must exist that makes matter clump together to form everything around us today. His theory hinged on the existence of a so-called "God Particle." While his ideas were good, they couldn't be proven. Until now.

In July of 2013, with the eighty-four-year-old Higgs sitting in the lecture hall, the European Organization for Nuclear Research announced that Higgs's theory as a young man in Edinburgh, Scotland, was indeed true. All along, he'd been right. The resulting emotion from the very British and stoic physicist was inspiring. He tried to hide it, but he was clearly moved to tears upon hearing that his theory had been proved and as he received praise from the scientists around him. "I was about to burst into tears. I was knocked over by the wave of the reaction of the audience. Up until then I was holding back emotionally, but when the audience reacted I couldn't hold back any more. That's the only way I can explain it."[1]

What fascinates me about this story isn't really the science part, or whether it proves or disproves the existence of God. What fascinates me is the grit, determination, and long-suffering work ethic of Higgs. I'm speculating, but I wonder if he knew in the 1960s that the technology to prove his theory simply didn't exist yet. But Higgs had the long view. He knew his particle could be proven one day, so what did he do? He kept working. As a young physicist, he didn't pout like a child that no one was listening to him. He put his head down and theorized and theorized, researched and researched. He waited for the time his career would peak at just the right moment. And peak it did. That year he won the Nobel Prize for Physics and had his fifty-year-old theory proven in a room full of his peers. How's that for a good year?

My friend Donald was the first to tell me that as a young social entrepreneur, the best thing I can do is set myself up to "peak when I'm sixty." Now, if you're already sixty or close to it, take a cue from Peter Higgs and kick it back to your eighties if that helps. It's less about the age and more about the pacing. I'm surprised by how many times I have to remind myself of the wisdom of the tortoise and the hare: "Slow and steady wins the race."

Like Peter Higgs, pacing ourselves achieves two very important things.

1. It releases a lot of the pressure we have on our shoulders right now. Believing that we don't have to be at our absolute best in this moment helps us focus squarely on our actual life today. Today is about doing something small and doing it well. This is liberating.
2. It frames our life and work into long-game thinking, forcing us to strategize a mental map of where we want to be in year one, five, ten, and so forth. Our life doesn't just happen to us. You can envision and create a road map for long-term success.

People often think they should be further along than they are now. We often come to these conclusions by comparing ourselves to the lives of others. I know I do. It's human nature to notice what others are doing around us, but an obsession with it can be devastating. Here's how it plays out for me. Every so often, I'll get an email from someone that goes like this: "Wow, Justin, I've seen you've been doing x, y, or z. Awesome. Have you ever heard of [organization] or [writer]? They basically do the same thing you do and are really successful. Maybe you can learn from them."

When I'm at my best, I *can* learn something from them. But more often than not, every time I read that email, I just feel horrible about myself. I feel terrible because I start comparing the beginning of my journey with another person's middle or end. I compare another person's best attribute to my very worst. Comparing yourself to others will ruin you. It will end your dream before it can start. As Teddy Roosevelt once said, "Comparison is the thief of joy." It's amazing how true this is.

The comparison game steals your joy, halts your momentum, and brings your greatest insecurities to the forefront of your mind. It's important to learn the mental skill of acknowledging another person's success without letting it throw *you* off track. This takes discipline. It takes heartache. It takes the emotional capacity to see beyond what you're feeling in the now.

When I come across a story of someone who is more successful than me in something I care about, I repeat this to myself over and over: *They have their story, and I have mine. They have their story, and I have mine. They have their story . . .*

This quick mental exercise has helped me quell the anxiety of comparison. I hope you'll try it. I truly believe that despite the perceived success of someone else, if we can keep showing up, we'll eventually carve out a niche that fits us perfectly. It doesn't matter if it takes us ten years to do what someone else did in one year. The point is that we're doing it in the first place.

———

There is a funny cartoon of a group of people mingling at a party. Above each of their heads is a thought bubble that reads, *"I wonder what they are thinking of me?"*

This silly cartoon sheds light on the fact that, for the most part, people aren't thinking about *you*. They are thinking about *themselves*. This is frustrating, but it should also be liberating.

We all know humans can be quite narcissistic and self-serving. But the narcissism of others gives you license to take great risk and then fail miserably if need be.

When you fail, there is a high likelihood that most people aren't even paying attention. Most of us spend tremendous effort trying to avoid even the possibility of failure. I know I do. We are worried about missing the mark because we fear what people will think of us. This forces us to play it safe, limiting ourselves to the things we already do well. But the truth is, people aren't really thinking about you—at least not in the way you think they are.

Most likely, people trust you a lot more than you trust yourself. They think you are far more resilient than you actually may be. I've learned recently that people actually have more patience with me sometimes than I do with myself. This is a license to be bold.

Once you free yourself from constantly trying to impress others and embrace the possibility of failure, the suffocating walls of self-doubt will erode around you. While it's hard to accept, no one will ever care about your interests and projects in the way that you do. Use this to your advantage. Take risks, fail big, rinse and repeat.

Chapter 9

THE SLOW WORK OF GOD

*Remember that there is meaning beyond
absurdity. Be sure that every little deed
counts, that every word has power.
Never forget that you can still do your
share to redeem the world in spite of
all absurdities and frustrations and
disappointments.*

ABRAHAM JOSHUA HESCHEL

When I was twenty-three, I left the winter snowdrifts of
Grand Rapids, Michigan, for the torrential downpour of
Belfast, Northern Ireland. I've heard it said that if the weather
in Northern Ireland was better, there may have been a lot less

conflict. I can see the news headlines now: "The Peace Process and the Power of Vitamin D." A lot of Americans my age were too young to remember "the Troubles" in Northern Ireland and the ethnic conflict that pitted Catholics against Protestants in an urban war for identity, culture, and territory. As a result of the ongoing violence, Northern Ireland made international headlines for nearly three decades. Terrorist bombings, paramilitary shootings, and political turmoil branded a country the geographic size of Connecticut as a notorious place of division and bloodshed. I had an interest in conflict resolution and was eager to explore a place I'd studied in college, so an opportunity to work with students at the Presbyterian Chaplaincy at Queen's University Belfast was a dream come true.

At the time, Northern Ireland was officially in its post-conflict stage. Economic and social development had brought crucial disarmament treaties and warring political factions together in historic elections. The bullets and bombs had more or less subsided since the 1998 Good Friday agreement, but reconciliation on the ground, especially in working-class communities, was another matter altogether.

I'll never forget when my soon-to-be boss, a Presbyterian minister named Steve Stockman, picked me up from the airport for the first time and drove me through the green countryside on our way to my new home in the leafy suburbs of South Belfast. Getting off the freeway, we headed through Sandy Row, a Protestant paramilitary stronghold near the Belfast city center. A bright blue mural of a hooded gunman welcomed visitors to Sandy Row with massive text that read, *"You are now entering Loyalist Sandy Row, Heartland of South Belfast, Ulster Freedom Fighters."* We drove past the menacing mural with me

MADE FOR THESE TIMES

pinned to the window like a child on a driving tour of a Skittles factory. Once I saw that mural and the guns, I was hooked.

Well beyond the typical American fascination with all things Irish, I dove headfirst into the culture of Belfast, spoke with a Northern Irish lilt, and spent my weekends exploring the neighborhoods of Irish legend: IRA strongholds and paramilitary battlegrounds, murals of hooded men and looming weapons. The rioting in September of 2005 excited me to no end—I got to witness the carnage of political and sectarian violence firsthand. It was sick and twisted, I know, but coming from the sandy coast of California, the whirring sounds of police helicopters headed toward conflict zones drew me in like a tractor beam.

It's safe to say that Steve was quite surprised by my obsession with the darker side of Belfast. He used to say, "Fella, it seems you're a lot more interested in the things the devil has made than what God has made." He was right—or "dead on," as you'd say.

As my politics, values, and worldview began to develop, I longed to get my hands dirty. My work in Northern Ireland became my pride and joy. I spent late nights with Protestant college students in University residence halls dreaming of a better world, all the while spending my afternoons with working-class Catholic youth at a local community center.

It was one of my first days at the Mornington Community Project on the Lower Ormeau Road, a small Catholic enclave in the otherwise Protestant South Belfast. The Catholics in the area around the Mornington Project are a proud but cautious people, as they have suffered a handful of sectarian attacks on their community by neighboring Protestants. Mornington employs neighborhood residents in their cafe, holds trauma support groups and job training seminars, and runs extensive cross-community youth programs. The center's transformative efforts in South Belfast have impacted countless lives and represented a beacon of hope for the community.

One afternoon we had so many kids in the after-school program that I took about fifteen of them out early to play soccer to keep them from distracting the others. The boys were eager to introduce me to their neighborhood, and we stopped in a graffiti-covered alley where they showed me their artwork and taggings. Twelve-year-old Sean was very proud of the British Union Jack flag bursting into flames he had drawn. He beamed with pride as I acknowledged his artistic efforts. We played soccer in a vacant lot enclosed in graffiti and barbed wire. They scoured it beforehand, looking for loose change while I cleared broken glass. One boy lit up a half cigarette he found on the ground. He smoked it arrogantly while the others looked on with envy.

The fact that I was pretty good at soccer and had an impressive understanding of the English Premier League made me instantly credible with the Catholic boys from the Mornington Project. I tried to play it cool, but my heart soared when I overheard one of the older boys mutter, in the greatest working-class Irish accent ever, "Get in, the Yank knows his football, eh?"

That afternoon I scored a few goals (so what if the kids were twelve!), broke up a few fights, and tore a quarter-sized hole in my Vans sneakers. It was just about dark when some of the boys' mothers came and found us playing in the vacant lot. I was sweaty, and I hunched over, huffing in Belfast's cool autumn air as I introduced myself to tell them I'd be working at the

Mornington Project for the year. They deciphered my accent and appearance skeptically while one of the mothers, dragging her son away from the group, asked earnestly if I'd please "do ya best to keep me boys out of trouble."

———

I trudged up the steep stairs to Ken Humphrey's office, the director of the Mornington Project. Despite some success early on, the work had become increasingly difficult. The youth program was totally out of control. There had been expensive items stolen from the center, fights were breaking out, kids were vandalizing nearly everything, and I was tired of reprimanding teens for smoking cigarettes in the computer lab. The staff was exhausted, and I began to question if what we were doing was even making a difference.

Ken is a Protestant who chose to move his Protestant family sixteen years prior to the Catholic neighborhood to serve its people. As expected, certain Catholic groups in the area were skeptical of the Protestant involvement in the Mornington center. But because of the project's effectiveness, it was deemed worthy enough to stay in operation.

Ken said the secret to both their sanity and the success of Mornington had been that he had said "yes" to God's call and then just kept showing up. Day in, day out, over and over, he got out of bed, ate breakfast, and walked through the neighborhood to the center. Stopping to talk to the same people on the way, slowly but surely he built the trust needed to both survive and thrive in a place very few people like him would consider living and working.

Pretty soon it became habitual to have his Protestant family in the Catholic neighborhood. People saw the great work the center was doing in providing job training, counseling, youth programs, and economic empowerment. Ken told me that like him, no matter what, I had to dig deep to find my grit and keep showing up regardless of the outcome. He told me God was at work in this neighborhood. While God could easily change the hearts and minds of people on his own, God's preference is to work through the lives of people like me to move us inch by inch toward heaven on earth.

One day, Ken mentioned the need for a new art room. He suggested the kids begin learning to transfer some of their "artistic skills" from the outside walls of the Mornington building to more traditional artistic methods, for instance, paper. An American group was coming to Belfast on a conflict resolution trip, so I solicited their help in transforming a former storage room into something we could work with. We cleared out the old desks and boxes and then painted the walls a nice sunshine yellow.

With the room cleared and ready, over the next three weeks I brought seven Protestant art students from Queen's University down to the Mornington Project to help the kids paint murals on the walls to liven up the room. The artists worked with the kids early on to decide what type of images they wanted for their space. Then we used projectors to blow up drawings into full-size stencils of Irish dancers, soccer players, a snooker (billiards) player, and my personal favorite, a huge, shirtless torso of rapper Tupac Shakur. Seriously, Tupac's "thug life" stomach tattoo and everything. It was incredible.

Not only was this a fun project for both children and

volunteers, but it was an important cross-community event as well. Protestant artists would rarely if ever spend time in working-class Catholic neighborhoods and most likely harbored some apprehension about visiting the area. But I think the impact of this small cross-community project is even more significant coming from the other side. We had Catholic kids who were just beginning to realize that their new artist friends were Protestants who had very generously taken time out of their busy schedules to paint murals with them. This messed with their wee little heads. While they may have gone home at night and heard friends and family saying nasty things about the "Prod bastards" up the road, the hope was that the children would realize that the enemy was real people. They had names and personalities, and they were now their friends.

As I walked home after the art project, hands and forearms stained with paint, I began to truly believe that God moves in stealth ways unbeknown to us. It's what Father Greg Boyle calls "the slow work of God." It's the way we say yes, show up, put one foot in front of the other, and let God do the rest. Grit in action. Or as Boyle says, "You work, you hope, and you wait, for the light—this astonishing light."[1]

This astonishing light doesn't come from us. We are not responsible for creating or holding it. Our only job is to reflect it and to be in a constant state of reflection. The astonishing light comes from God in us as we reflect it onto others. If we're lucky, we'll see the way the light moves and grows in small actions we make over time. The choice for people like Ken to move into the Catholic neighborhood to work at Mornington. The Protestant volunteers who chose to venture into an unknown neighborhood a handful of times to paint murals when they probably had better things to do. The kids' decisions to go to Mornington every day to get their homework done. My choice to slog through the wet Belfast winter to be present at Mornington when I didn't feel like it. It's all these small decisions coupled with God's unyielding grace that softens all of our hearts for people who are different than us.

The slow work of God.

Chapter 10

THE BONFIRE

*What can we gain by sailing to the moon
if we are not able to cross the abyss that
separates us from ourselves?*

———

THOMAS MERTON

I'd been living with my boss, Steve, and his family in Belfast, but they had left for the rest of the summer to their vacation home in Ballycastle, a tiny beach village on the north coast of Northern Ireland. Students and friends had gone home for the summer, and the University district was vacant. I found myself most days alone in the empty house, bored, depressed, missing my then-girlfriend and now wife, Trisha. I knew it was bad when I would lie on the floor of the kitchen listening to Snow

Patrol's "Set Fire to the Third Bar" on repeat, acting out the brutal heartache of the lyrics.

Snow Patrol were from Belfast, and their record *Eyes Open* had jumped into pop significance that year, all the while tearing me apart from the inside out. Listening to it now, more than a decade later, still sends a chill down my spine. I ached for my Northern Irish friends who had left town and even more so for the loved ones I had back home. Even though I was an outsider in every sense of the word, for that final month, the Mornington Project became my family.

I was upstairs in the Mornington office when Mary, one of the administers, said, "Justin, we've heard from some of the kids you've been invited to the bonfire tonight."

It was true. I had been invited and was very honored by it. August 9 marks the anniversary of Irish Internment, an important day in history for many in the Catholic Community. In August of 1971 the British Government launched *Operation Demetrius*, a highly controversial military operation where they arrested hundreds of Catholics accused of paramilitary activity around Northern Ireland. During the operation, the British Army killed ten civilians and detained 342 people, leading to widespread protests and rioting. Every August, Catholics in working-class communities around Northern Ireland commemorate Internment with huge bonfires and occasional paramilitary displays.

The community support for these bonfires has dwindled over recent years due to their highly sectarian nature, underage alcohol consumption, and the fact that teenagers were building fifty-foot inferno towers in urban areas. Still, for many in these communities, the bonfires are local traditions not often accessible to outsiders.

Mary mentioned that none of the Mornington staff were going to attend the bonfire, and she asked if I wouldn't mind looking out for the building while I was there. I stared at her quizzically.

"Well, you know, Justin, they build the bonfire in the vacant lot next door, but last year, it was built too high, and a big piece of it toppled over and almost lit our building on fire. Thankfully, a few of the kids were able to put it out. So this year, I expect you to be able to take care of things if something were to go wrong."

Not only was I worried about being an outsider at a community event centered around fire and sectarianism, but it was also now my job to take care of the center if something were to happen involving a three-story bonfire.

"If things get out of hand, shouldn't I just call the fire brigade?" I asked.

"No, no, no," Mary responded. "Don't call the fire brigade if it's the last thing you do. They'll throw stones at the fire brigade. You know these kids well enough by now. This community doesn't trust the police or fire brigade. That'll do more harm than good. You'll have to just take care of it on your own."

I prayed on the floor of my room before leaving for the bonfire. Was I really doing this? I dressed in all black and wore my running shoes, just in case. I was beyond nervous. Would I be accepted? What if the center goes up in flames? I knew a lot of the older, harder guys from the community would be there, possibly some local paramilitaries. I was really anxious someone would say, "Who are you? You're not from here." Could I outrun them?

I saw the bonfire in the reflections of storefront windows before I saw the real thing. Turning the corner into the estate, the inferno was raging. It was some twenty-five feet high, stacked with wood pallets and old tires. British Union Jacks and Protestant paramilitary flags hung burning from it. The crowd cheered when a new flag went up in flames.

I approached apprehensively and luckily walked right into a group of kids from the Mornington Project. "Justin! You came! Look, guys, Justin came to the bonfire!" The kids crowded around, giddy with excitement to show off the fiery creation they'd spent the last two weeks building. They picked up scrap wood and rocks, hurling them into the blaze, bragging about stealing the flags from the adjacent Protestant neighborhood the evening before. A few of the older teenagers came over to say hi. One shook my hand, saying, "Thanks for coming. We didn't think you'd show." The simple act of showing up trumped the fact that I was an outsider, not to mention a Protestant.

Ciara, one of the older teens who volunteered at the center, said that they'd never had an American come to a bonfire before. I beamed with pride. Some of the parents of kids from Mornington came around to say hi or reintroduce themselves, including the mothers from the soccer game on the first day. I had committed myself to this community for the year, and even though I was set to leave in less than a month, they accepted me and made me feel welcome. For the first time in a while, I felt whole.

To a Christian and law-abiding citizen, a bonfire like this presents a lot of problems. There's the vibrant celebration of conflict, the underage drinking, and the glorification of sectarianism that has driven a wedge through this tiny country for decades. But on that night, it wasn't my job to judge. I was there to be present. Thankfully, the bonfire didn't topple over, and I didn't make the mistake of calling the fire brigade. I ran home afterward and stared at myself in the bathroom mirror in disbelief of the evening's events.

I made it a point to not tell Steve that I'd be attending the bonfire at Mornington. He and his lovely wife, Janice, were concerned I'd put myself in too many dangerous scenarios already. But I thought about what Steve preached time and time again to the students at the Presbyterian Chaplaincy. Steve broke down the gospel in the plainest form imaginable. He says Jesus speaks to us with two simple words: "Follow me."

The Christian message can get pretty convoluted nowadays. The various interpretations, the politics, the dos and don'ts, the fringe groups on all sides. But Steve just brushes all that off the table and goes back to the heart of it all: Jesus telling us, point blank, "Follow me." Followers envision the kingdom as it arrives and act like it's already here. Followers don't merely love Jesus; they try to act like him too. Steve taught me that following Jesus means that we walk to the places he would walk. We talk to the people he would talk to. It means we make his priorities our priorities. These types of values aren't dropped in as nice gestures or cute additions to the Christian life; this is *the* Christian life.

Time and time again in the Scriptures, we see that Jesus' heart, his "preferential option,"[1] is for the poor, the marginalized, the ill, and the forgotten. I began to wonder if a relationship with Christ alongside friendships with those who are suffering was in fact the clearest way to God. When Jesus talks about the kingdom of God, it's often centered on the ones least likely to receive it, like the time Jesus told a bunch of religious leaders that the tax collectors and prostitutes would be entering heaven ahead of them. Yikes.

It may have been the adrenaline, but I can't deny that Jesus was there with me on that Monday night in August, pushing me forward to connect with a community I had very little in common with but needed. At the bonfire, I finally grasped that God is alive and well even in the midst of destruction. I didn't believe in the split between the sacred and the secular anymore but instead saw the world as DNA strands of good and evil weaving their way through all earthly places. It is a dangerous religious myth that God only resides at the altars of our churches or sunsets over sandy beaches; I found his presence literally on fire in places where evil supposedly reigns supreme.

My experience in Belfast helped me realize that this Jesus thing is messy. It's disorganized, confusing, and can't be pinned down to a formula for every person. But in the simplest of terms, our job is to follow him where he leads, one step in front of the other over time. Following Jesus isn't supposed to be some religious retreat or exotic holiday. It may be filled with hope and joy, but it's also raw, intense, and unsafe by nature.

As C. S. Lewis refers to Aslan in *The Lion, the Witch and the Wardrobe*, "'Safe?' said Mr. Beaver, 'who said anything about safe? 'Course He isn't safe. But He's good. He's the King.'"[2]

Theologian N. T. Wright says the job of a Christian is to create signposts pointing into the mist—signposts that show the direction of the kingdom of God, even though we're not actually able to see the whole thing. Forty miles south of Belfast, the rough wooden signs marking trailheads to the Mourne Mountains don't hint at the stunning valley you'll find at the end, but as Wright notes, "that doesn't mean they aren't pointing in the right direction."[3]

Living in Belfast all those years ago, I often felt like my faith wasn't "feeling" the way it is "supposed" to feel. And that would usually make me sad and guilty, until I finally realized that it's simply okay to feel messy and disconnected. No matter what we do, God can't love us any less. On the contrary, we are loved and named and known by a God who is inviting us to join him in the restoration of the world. And it's a tedious job, which is why this revolutionary gospel has to be based on grace—a scandalous and unfair type of grace that makes no sense. It's the kind that promises no matter how dirty and vile we are on the inside, Jesus will let us off the hook if we promise to follow him. When we round the corners of the neighborhoods on the wrong side of the tracks, we'll find him waiting for us, hammering in signposts. He'll say, "There you are. I've been waiting for you. Forget about what you've done. I already have. Let me grab you a hammer."

You aren't
ALONE
ON THIS
journey...

Part IV | THE COMPANIONS

There is a reason Harry Potter and Frodo Baggins were destined to save the world. They were brave, humble, and clever, but they also had friends who would follow them to the ends of the earth.

In times of the most intense fog, the companions we journey with make all the difference. You aren't alone in this.

Relationships matter. They make us who we are. And it's who you are, not what you do, that rallies people around you. It's the people closest to you who help magnify the meaning in your life.

The Zulu word for this is *ubuntu*, the South African philosophy of interconnectedness, a belief system in which all people are beautifully bound up together. Popularized by Archbishop Desmond Tutu, ubuntu is the belief in the woven tapestry of our humanity. I am me because of you, and injustice against one is an injustice against all.

You might have the most impressive ideas and work ethic in the world, but I don't think you'll be truly successful until you can get a handful of people at your kitchen table who say they trust you. Because regardless of our personal ambition, it's in the talents of others around us, woven together with ours, that help us reach our full potential. No man is an island.

Seth Godin wrote a great little book called *Tribes* that aims to inspire new leaders to build tribes of people around them to accomplish great things. The tagline of the book is, "We need you to lead us." I love that.

If you have a good idea or vision of any kind, we desperately need you to lead us. But I'm not going to follow unless there is something in you that I trust. The positive impact of people with poor character is fleeting. Over time, one person's inner darkness can put an entire company, church, mission, or family at risk. It may not happen right away, but like the low tide, eventually everyone around them will start to retreat, with only jagged rocks left for all to see.

I've heard it described this way: character is how you treat people who can do nothing for you. I'm talking about the people throughout your day who you can gloss over without even meaning to. In human relationships, the small stuff matters. A million tiny droplets of rain can both grow a forest and cause a landslide.

People who build and maintain great relationships are the ones who change the world. They can embolden others, shape families, save lives, and inspire organizations. We need companions in this life.

The following chapters provide a road map for the power of human relationships. We'll explore how to prioritize our character, constrain the impact of technology, harness our humility, and use empathy to drive our calling forward.

Let's dive in.

Chapter 11

STARVE THE EGO,
FEED THE SOUL

*Nobody's better than me, but I'm no better
than anyone else.*

———

DAVID BROOKS

I'm fascinated by funerals. Morbid, I know. The white gloves. The weight of the casket. What is said and what is omitted. How to consolidate the celebration of a human life in a sixty-minute program. I'm also fascinated by the stories you hear every so often where at the last moment, a funeral has to be moved to a larger venue because more guests than expected turn up. What a surprise that must be to a grieving family. It's a beautiful confirmation of a life well lived. I'm curious what type of life results in a "standing room only" final day. What are the qualities of a person whose guests fill the overflow room?

In his book *The Road to Character*, David Brooks creates a distinction between our "résumé virtues" and our "eulogy virtues." Résumé virtues are the skills, achievements, and abilities that help us advance a career and find success. Eulogy virtues, by contrast, are what people say about you at your funeral. These are the ways people describe who you really were, the depths of your character, and the impact you had on others.

Another way to describe it is from Rabbi Joseph Soloveitchik's book, *Lonely Man of Faith*. Soloveitchik categorizes the two opposing sides to our humanity as Adam I and Adam II. Adam I is career-oriented and ambitious. He wants to build, discover, achieve, and win. Adam II, on the other hand, is about obeying a calling and serving the world. He is focused on his integrity, his role in humanity, and the depths of his morality.

The distinction between our inner Adam I and Adam II shouldn't come as a surprise, yet one is clearly harder to cultivate than the other. As David Brooks describes,

> We all know our eulogy virtues are more important than the résumé ones. But our culture and our educational systems spend more time teaching the skills and strategies you need for career success than the qualities you need to radiate that sort of inner light. Many of us are clearer on how to build an external career than on how to build inner character.[1]

I believe one of the greatest tests we face is how to manage the tension between our résumé virtues and eulogy virtues, the battle between our ego and our soul. This is a daily struggle, a constant tug-of-war in our innermost being that will define what type of person you are and will be. Let me be clear, this tension isn't wrong. Trying to find a harmonious balance between two, sometimes opposing worldviews is difficult. And it shows we're paying attention. But how you manage this tension will not only determine how effective you'll be as a friend, spouse, parent, and leader, but it will define your role in God's redemption of the world.

———

Sean and James were two of my favorite kids at the Mornington Center in Belfast. One day, I asked James if they were still fighting with the "wee orangies" (loyalist Protestants) across the road. He replied that it happened every once in a while and followed his remarks with a handful of sectarian obscenities and accounts of how *they* continued to terrorize *his* neighborhood. I asked him if he remembered that I had caught him only a few days prior throwing stones with some other boys over the railroad tracks into the Protestant neighborhood. He smiled bashfully, admitting that perhaps the wee orangies weren't always the perpetrators.

I decided to take our conversation to a place I never initially intended it to go. The bulk of Northern Irish society still enforces segregated schools and neighborhoods, so while I already knew the answer to my question, I asked James if he had ever talked to any of the boys from across the railroad tracks. As expected, he confessed he hadn't and restated his position with a few more bigoted comments. I then asked

James how he would feel if he found out there were Protestants who were secretly coming to the Mornington club. His eyes tripled in size as he exclaimed, "What!? If there were orangies at this club, well, me and Sean we'd kick their faces in. This is our club, they aren't allowed."

I smiled at his venomous response and calmly told him that I happened to be a Protestant and was in Northern Ireland working for a Protestant church.

He quickly caught Sean's eye across the room and shouted, "Sean, did you know Justin is a Prod?!" Until this moment I was unsure if Sean even knew. We'd been hanging out for months now, but it never came up.

Sean looked up from his homework and responded, "Ya, I know. I've known that since the first day. But he's our friend now. None of that other stuff matters if someone is your friend."

I believe only human relationships and the grace of God have the power to change hearts and minds. Only through friendship can we challenge opinions and rewire entrenched worldviews. Sean accepted me, and I him, even though I was a Prod.

Heineken, the Dutch beer company, put out a video where two participants who didn't know each other worked together on a small building project. They followed instructions to align connecting slabs of wood until they had constructed a small bar to sit at together. Then the screens behind them high-lighted videos of the participants sharing deeply held beliefs on controversial political topics: race, gay rights, climate change, and more. In that moment, the participants realized the person they were just working alongside held the extreme opposite viewpoint from their own. Heineken then gave them a choice. They could leave the set or share a beer at the bar they'd just built together. All the participants choose to stay, and from the foundation of a newfound friendship, they began sharing in healthy dialogue.

We live in divided times. The politics of race, religion, and global economics create divisions between rich and poor, north and south, red and blue. As I've learned again and again, people with character are the ones willing to cross dividing lines. People committed to their eulogy virtues don't surround themselves only with people who look like, talk like, and always agree with them. As Jesus said, "If you love those who love you, what credit is that to you? Even sinners love those who love them. And if you do good to those who are good to you, what credit is that to you? Even sinners do that" (Luke 6:32–33).

One of my heroes is a guy named Daryl Davis. He's not an actor, athlete, or some Fortune 500 CEO. He's a musician who in the early part of his life played piano with blues legends like Chuck Berry and Jerry Lee Lewis. But it's Daryl's peculiar hobby outside of music that has garnered him national recognition recently. In his spare time, Daryl, who is black, befriends Ku Klux Klan members and white supremacists. Using both music and his superior relationship skills, Daryl travels around the country attending neo-Nazi rallies and sitting down over beers with Imperial Wizards of the KKK.

Daryl isn't a part of an organization or on some political mission. He's just a really good piano player who realized one day that the only way to do something about race relations in America was to insert himself directly into the gaze of the people who supposedly hate him the most. The results have been staggering. Over the course of three decades, Daryl has personally helped two hundred Klan members renounce their membership in the KKK. Many of them actually gave Daryl their Klan robes and hoods as symbols of their decision to leave white supremacist organizations. In the PBS documentary about Daryl's life, *Accidental Courtesy*, Daryl shows off the dozens upon dozens of Klan robes he has stacked up in his closet. "I never set out to convert anyone in the Klan. I just set out to get an answer to my question, 'How can you hate me when you don't even know me?' I simply gave them a chance to get to know me and treat them the way I want to be treated. They come to their own conclusion that this ideology is no longer for them."[2]

Black, white, or brown. Left, right, or center. Catholic, Protestant, Muslim, Buddhist, agnostic, or atheist. We all desire to belong. Daryl Davis knows this and reminds us how courageous relationships change lives. Daryl could have easily allowed his life's legacy to stay firmly planted in the realm of his résumé virtues. Chart-topping hits, nationwide tours, and screaming fans would be immeasurably satisfying for many of us. But Daryl is made for something more. He was created by God to take his hard skills as a musician and use them to write a greater song, one that sings of hope and reconciliation. Daryl's efforts at changing the hearts and minds of white supremacists is what people will talk about at his funeral. His music career is simply the soundtrack in the background.

———

My friend Sarah Thebarge was only twenty-eight when she was

diagnosed with breast cancer. Her eighteen months of treatment included five surgeries, six months of chemo, and thirty sessions of radiation, not to mention the pneumonia and the sepsis.

While in recovery, she was riding the light rail into Portland when she saw two sets of tiny brown eyes peek around the corner of her book. What started as a game of peek-a-boo turned into a conversation with a mother from Somalia and her two daughters. She didn't realize it at the time (we rarely do), but Sarah had just walked into her moment of obligation. God had given her an opportunity to say yes or no.

As she arrived at her destination, she was given a choice. Would she figure out a way to see the girls again, or would she get off the train, go to work, and continue to live her life as she intended?

Sarah chose the former. She took down their address and promised to visit soon. In her subsequent visits she dove deeper into relationship with the girls, their families, and the Somali community in Portland. The relationships became so powerful, Sarah would write a best-selling book about them called *The Invisible Girls*. The success of the book meant she could start a scholarship fund for the girls. She then started traveling around the country telling their story, sharing with anyone who would listen about the hope and adversity of refugees and immigrants in America.

A moment of obligation on the train gave Sarah the opportunity to reveal her true character. The pain of her past could have made her turn inward and bitter. But instead she turned outward. She allowed the difficulty of her own experiences to soften her toward the suffering of others. Many might laud her résumé virtues—her Ivy League degree, a successful nursing career, the number of books she's sold. But I am far more impressed by her dogged advocacy for vulnerable people. I am inspired by her ability to say "Yes" when many would have said "Not now."

When people talk about Sarah, they talk about the way she loves people, the way the light of Christ is so intense inside of her that she can't help but reflect it to others. These are the eulogy virtues that set her apart as a beacon for good in this world.

Sarah isn't a world-renowned nurse, and Daryl Davis isn't in the Rock and Roll Hall of Fame. But they are both the type of people who will have their funerals moved at the last minute for the thousands of people who will show up out of nowhere. Sarah and Daryl personify the idea of starving the ego to feed the soul. They've skillfully and systematically put their egos in check to invest in others and fulfill the deep longings of their souls. As a result, both are people other people want to follow and are drawn to. Their character gives them the authority to lead.

Author Simon Sinek reminds us how "leaders eat last." Sinek says the best leaders put others before themselves and in turn are "rewarded with deeply loyal colleagues who will stop at nothing to advance the leader's vision." While not the ultimate goal, the focus on our character can have a profound effect. The more we give to others in our organization, community, or family, the more they'll give back to us.

It's nearly impossible to kill off your ego, but like Sarah and Daryl, you can starve it into submission. And when it's starved and tempered, you can use it for good. Our résumé virtues, the ambition and drive from Adam I, are not inherently bad. But if we live primarily for external achievement, years can pass with the deepest parts of ourselves untouched. Without meaning to, we begin to lose our moral vocabulary. As David Brooks writes,

> It is easy to slip into a self-satisfied moral mediocrity. You grade yourself on a forgiving curve. You figure as long as you are not obviously hurting anybody and people seem to like you, you must be O.K. But you live with an unconscious boredom, separated from the deepest meaning of life and the highest moral joys. Gradually, a humiliating gap opens between your actual self and your desired self, between you and those incandescent souls you sometimes meet.[3]

If you've found yourself convicted by the way you've focused on your résumé virtues at the expense of your eulogy ones, don't be discouraged. Take heart, our ambitions and their external applications have the potential to put us in scenarios where our eulogy virtues can shine. Capitalize on these opportunities. We can have ambition. But to what end? We can aspire to be leaders. But what type of leader will you be? The Bible is full of kings, rulers, and commanders who are blessed and empowered by God to lead nations and grow movements. But the goal should be harnessing the depths of your soul to work toward a noble and worthy quest.

I believe the cultivation of our inner life, our sanctuary life, can make us more effective and stronger out in a world dominated by our résumé virtues. We can weather storms, dig deeper, and push harder. We can grow companies, start movements, empower families, and promote ideas that glorify goodness and truth. A deep connection to our souls, coupled with character and tempered ambition, can make us far more effective leaders, builders, and changemakers. Furthermore, it allows us to invite others in a larger, more meaningful journey.

Chapter 12

THE DESIRE TO MATTER

Before I was married, I lived with four roommates in a run-down house off 84th and Foster Avenue in southeast Portland. When George, Sam, Blair, Scotty, and I moved in, the yard was covered in trash, the roof and fence sagged, and our negligent landlord had stuffed newspaper in the corners of the single-pane windows that had been broken over the years. Well before the economy rebounded and waves of gentrification hit Portland, the neighborhood was aptly named "Felony Flats" due to high crime rates along Portland's then-infamous 82nd Avenue.

Our little crew of idealists had moved out of downtown and specifically into that house to work in nearby schools and serve the neighborhood the best we could. I ran These Numbers Have Faces out of the attic during all hours of the night with furniture and office supplies from a nearby thrift store. Out back, my roommate Sam spent his time working on his motorcycle and roasting coffee in a rickety old shed he had cleaned out. He started roasting first with popcorn makers and later a cheap coffee roaster he bought on Craigslist. We wouldn't have guessed it back then, but Sam is now a successful Portland restaurateur. His trendy shop Good Coffee is a mainstay for the hip creatives of southeast Portland.

We were so frugal that one winter we couldn't justify the cost of fuel for the oil furnace. For nearly six months, we layered on hoodies and scarves while huddled separately in our rooms around space heaters, waiting in agony for summertime. My friend Chas from California came to Portland that February to be my first-ever intern at These Numbers Have Faces. The first morning in our house, he poured coffee into his favorite mug, which was now ice cold from a night in our kitchen, and watched it shatter into a thousand pieces when the hot coffee hit it.

Aiming to do something small but meaningful, we set up a soccer goal and basketball hoop outside on the street. Within a month, our dilapidated house became ground zero for groups of neighborhood kids. After meeting their parents and earning their trust, the five of us invested heavily, day after day, in the lives of the kids on our street. We helped with homework and played video games. We hosted basketball and soccer games until dark, and we took kids on field trips outside the city to places they'd never been.

For a while, it was a blast. Then we walked outside to see kids sleeping on the porch to avoid going home, uncovered drugs in backpacks, and had stuff stolen from our house. One afternoon, I found myself driving to Juvenile Hall to be a character witness for a neighborhood kid after he was expelled from middle school for assaulting a teacher. We weren't licensed social workers or trained child advocates. We had no boundaries and no idea what we were doing. All we had was the daily slog of a commitment the five of us had made to each other and the neighborhood. For me, our little mission, however misguided, was another opportunity to do right by my experience with Malik back in Michigan.

One of the boys on the street, Michael, became one of our most frequent visitors. Like a lot of the boys in our neighborhood, his dad has been incarcerated most of Michael's life. His mom was working two jobs, so Michael and his brother started coming over to our house nearly every day after school. One day Michael informed us he had a basketball game at the local Boys and Girls Club and asked if we'd be able to attend. It was a Tuesday night, and we had a full agenda planned for our weekly house meeting. But after eating, we decided that instead of talking about our role in the neighborhood, we'd go and support Michael.

Showing up at halftime, we saw Michael in the middle of the huddle. He looked up, saw us, and beamed. Like a man possessed, he went on to score twenty points in the second half. After the game he bounded toward our group smiling ear to ear and explained how no one had ever come to see him play before.

I find myself looking back on these years with a sneer of cynicism. A group of well-meaning twentysomethings moved into a neighborhood we weren't from to try and do something good now reeks of yet another thoughtless social justice blunder. Just a few years after we started, we all got married, moved away, and once again abandoned the kids we set out to help.

Every once in a while, I'll be out on that side of town and drive by our old house to marvel at a neighborhood transformed. Depending on your perspective of urban development, it's surreal to see what were once vacant lots now home to upscale shops and sparkling new condos.

Back then, I really wanted people to think I was super smart. So I'd buy famous and important books and bend the bindings a bunch so it looked like I had read them a ton of times, even though I hadn't. It was remarkably petty and stupid. To this day, on my bookshelf sit all the greats from famous Russian novelists, like *Crime and Punishment, The Brothers Karamazov, War and Peace,* and *Anna Karenina.* They are as artificial as a trophy displayed but never won.

I faked my way toward intellectualism, but Fyodor Dostoyevsky (the author of some of those books I've never read) spent his days being punished for it. Dostoyevsky was imprisoned for six years for his role in a Russian intellectual group called the Petrashevsky Circle. The group was highly critical of Tsar Nicholas, so they were rounded up and sentenced to death in 1849. But instead of actually killing them, the Russian troops did a mock execution and sent them to hard labor in Siberia. While in the prison camp, Dostoyevsky discovered something fascinating about human nature. He concluded, "Human beings are not driven by self-interest, but by an insatiable desire to matter, to leave their mark, to be heard—even if all they say is a curse."[1]

There couldn't be a more terrible place on earth than a labor camp in Siberia. Yet Dostoyevsky reminds us that even when humans are at their lowest point, the place closest to their death, they still desire to be valued, to matter, and to leave a legacy.

As I've reflected on my time with the neighborhood kids in Felony Flats, I began to detect the same thread in nearly every experience I've had across the world. From Belfast to Rwanda, Grand Rapids to Portland, the desire to matter is paramount. Everyone wants it, and most don't get nearly enough of it. Yet we all possess the potential to provide it for others, which in turn helps us to find it in ourselves. Even if it's misguided or temporary, I've begun to believe that fulfilling someone's "insatiable desire to matter" is actually fundamental to human flourishing. Our investment in others has the potential to be the surest way to our own satisfaction.

———

Jesus didn't need the twelve disciples by his side for his mission on earth to flourish. He could have easily healed the sick, restored the sight of the blind, and agitated the religious and political leaders of his day all by himself. Think Bruce Willis in *Die Hard*. Why use the police when they are a bunch of bumbling idiots? Go solo. Instead, Jesus chose to surround himself with twelve companions, all of them flawed, to invest in, challenge, and become the future mouthpiece for the largest spiritual movement in human history.

In Mark 4 we see Jesus come alongside the twelve disciples in a unique way that reveals a glimpse of his character and humility. Often speaking in metaphor, Jesus shared the parable of the sower, which is about the Word of God being scattered like seeds into various landscapes. Like his stories often did, Jesus' story left the disciples confused. Despite their confusion, Jesus responds gracefully. I love the way *The Message* translation describes it. "With many stories like these, he presented his message to them, fitting the stories to their experience and maturity. He was never without a story when he spoke. When he was alone with his disciples, he went over everything, sorting out the tangles, untying the knots" (Mark 4:33–34 The Message).

"Sorting out the tangles, untying the knots." This is a very simple, often overlooked description of the character of Jesus. I envision him hunched over, leaning into his disciples, explaining again and again what these stories really mean. We often forget that the twelve disciples were simple people. They were predominantly uneducated, manual laborers. Many of these metaphors and allegories would truly be difficult for them to grasp. But there is Jesus, explaining it again, his reassuring hand on their shoulder, untying the knots of their minds.

While he didn't need to, Jesus is the ultimate example of someone who chose to bind up his humanity in others. He is the deepest expression of humility and character. As people made for these times, we must ask ourselves if we are willing to humble ourselves like Christ. Are we willing to help others feel like they matter? No matter our age, career path, social standing, or the amount of money we have in the bank, are we willing to sit with people and untie the knots?

———

In 2014, These Numbers Have Faces launched the Accelerate Academy, a two-year business incubator to coach, train, and invest in the next generation of East African entrepreneurs. We've always been firm believers in education, but we have also known it is entrepreneurs who build the economies of the future. If East Africa was to solve their own challenges and create shared prosperity for all, they needed young people to start enterprises that employed others and boosted the local economy.

Whether in the first world or third world, entrepreneurship is a risky endeavor. I've read that 80 percent of small businesses started in the United States fail within the first eighteen months.[2] The data is similar if not higher in East Africa. But in our research of how to build a successful business accelerator, we came across a unique realization: we learned entrepreneurs are far more likely to succeed when they have a mentor. According to the U.S. Small Business Association, businesses that receive just three or more hours of mentoring achieve higher revenues and increased business growth.[3] Even better, according to a 2014 survey by the UPS Store, 70 percent of small businesses that receive mentoring survive more than five years—double the survival rate of nonmentored businesses.[4]

With this knowledge in hand and These Numbers Have Faces already a deeply people-centered organization, we set out to build the most relationship driven business accelerator in East Africa. From hundreds of applications online, we choose the top 100–150 young entrepreneurs to attend the annual Accelerate Summit—a three-day conference with dozens of local and international coaches in attendance. Nothing gives me more joy than walking around the Accelerate Summit and seeing local coaches working with small groups of entrepreneurs perfecting their business plans, going over their finances, and polishing their elevator pitches. I get to witness in real life the "sorting out the tangles and untying the knots," exactly as Christ modeled for his disciples.

On the final day of the Summit, we choose the most promising thirty to fifty entrepreneurs to join the full Accelerate Academy. As their names are announced, the selected few whoop and holler as they run onto the stage. Some break down in tears; others beam as they call their parents to break the good news. The mentoring doesn't stop. Eight more months of in-depth coaching all lead up to the Accelerate Finale Pitch Event where impact investors fly to Rwanda to hear about their businesses and provide game-changing investments to scale their enterprises.

The Accelerate Academy started with a crazy idea in our US office and a humble 2014 Accelerate Summit in a tiny lecture hall at a Rwandan university. But the relationship-based model has stayed consistent. Since our simple beginnings, the program has gone on to mentor hundreds of entrepreneurs and place tens of thousands of dollars into their businesses.

From tech startups to banana farmers, green energy to water delivery, Accelerate entrepreneurs have employed hundreds of their fellow Rwandans, transforming the lives of thousands of people. The mentoring model continues as our alumni come back to coach year after year, further investing in the young people behind them. Relationships change lives. They fulfil our deepest desire to matter, and they sort out the tangles and untie the knots, reflecting the light of God within us.

Chapter 13

YOU CAN'T DIGITIZE FISHING

*What greater thing is there for human
souls than to feel they are joined for
life—to be with each other in silent,
unspeakable memories.*

———

GEORGE ELIOT

I've lived in the Pacific Northwest for twelve years now.
While not a fisherman myself, it's common knowledge that
for salmon and steelhead, the Northwest is one of the best fishing destinations in the entire world.

My friend Chris is an avid fly fisherman, and he once told
me, "You can't digitize fishing." No technological advance-
ment can replace the raw experience of fishing. Besides the

commercial kind, for individuals, fishing has remained nearly the exact same experience for thousands of years. Technology can't replicate the rod in your hands, the cool water running over your feet, the thrash of the fish, and the sense of accomplishment in finishing the fight. The sport of fishing requires a close-knit relationship with nature wherein one must be fully present to truly accomplish the task at hand.

I watched a video online of a social experiment in which a young girl pretended to be homeless to see how the general public would react and whether they would help her. You've probably seen these before. The end result didn't really surprise me as much as the number of people who walked by this child while staring at their phones. They didn't even give themselves the opportunity to make a decision whether to engage. Rather, they completely missed that anything was happening at all. They were oblivious. As Buddhist monk Thich Nhat Hanh says, "Once there is seeing, there must be acting. Otherwise, what is the use of seeing?"[1]

What worries me most is the way technology has the ability to distract us from both human relationships and compelling moments of obligation. Distracted by a phone or locked inside watching TV makes us far likelier to miss critical moments in our pursuit of purpose, ones that I believe God places in our path, hoping we'll be scanning for. We may blame companies and advertisers for how they impact our psyche, but I have an inkling there is something closer to our core that enables this.

The more I've reflected on how to build relationships and develop character, the more it's become clear that you can't digitize the process. Relationships are, by nature, frustratingly inefficient. They can't be streamlined in the ways the rest of our lives are. It's taken Daryl Davis thirty years to convince two hundred racists to renounce their membership in the KKK. There is no mobile application or virtual reality experience that can get the same results as Daryl sharing beers and talking face to face with a white supremacist over the course of three decades.

For people in the West who are accustomed to fast food, fast internet, and fast solutions to every problem, this can be aggravating. The benefits of character that forms from deep human relationships take years upon years to develop. They are coveted and desired because they are hard won. If they were easy, they would lose their significance.

———

During my first visit to Rwanda in 2012, while volunteering for a day at a health clinic, I met a young man about my own age smiling happily as we walked along a rural village road outside the capital city of Kigali.

"Why are you smiling?" I asked.

His smile got even larger. "Because yesterday, my village got electricity, and last night I charged my mobile phone while I slept!" He pulled a cheap, Chinese-made smartphone out of his pocket, the charger still dangling from it. "This one even has Facebook!" he exulted, before turning down a lonely road lined with banana trees.

Access to technology for the world's poorest people is one of the most powerful tools for global prosperity. Mobile phones and a 3G wireless connection have provided economic freedom and connection with loved ones in some of the most remote places in the world. Through my work with These Numbers Have Faces, few things give me more personal joy than texting with my African friends about European soccer. After the banter, I'll inevitably ask them where they are at that exact moment. Many will say, "I'm at home, in the refugee camp with my family," a place I know doesn't have running water, proper sanitation, and ironically electricity to even charge a mobile device. But a cheap smartphone and a 3G connection enables our friendly jabbing about Barcelona, Arsenal, and Manchester City.

For many of my friends in refugee camps, the technology is still novel and invigorating. They may not see the train pounding down the tracks headed directly toward them. Danger lies ahead.

Research shows today's young people, despite unparalleled access to technology, are the loneliest people alive today—even more lonely than the elderly, the majority of whom live alone. Young people have thousands of friends online but far fewer real connections to human beings. This loneliness isn't just sad; it's life threatening. Researchers are finding mounting evidence linking loneliness to physical illnesses, cognitive decline, and a greater predictor of early death than obesity.[2]

Scarier still are the new reports from an even younger generation, those who don't remember life before the ubiquitous takeover of the internet and smartphones. Unlike generations before them, today's teens and preteens drive less, drink less, party less, and date less. At first glance, the significant decrease in car accidents, alcohol related deaths, and unplanned pregnancies are perceived as overwhelmingly positive. But the newfound "safety" of today's teens and preteens is also due to the fact that they spend a staggering number of hours at home, alone, looking at their phones. *The Atlantic* reported that the number of teens who get together with their friends nearly every day dropped by more than 40 percent from 2000 to 2015. As a result, rates of teen depression and suicide have skyrocketed since 2011.[3]

Let me be clear. I believe wholeheartedly in the next generation of young people. They possess an unparalleled tenacity for the most challenging issues of our time and have leveraged technology as a mobilizing force for good. However, unless they can learn to temper the isolating dark side of technology addiction, this is a generation on the brink of the worst mental-health crisis in decades.

The irony here is astonishing. We have global access to more relationships and information than we know what to do with, but we find ourselves isolated and alone. We're living in a post-truth world with terabyte upon terabyte of information, and we can't discern what is fake or real. We are a culture drowning in data but starving for wisdom. As people made for these times, we're different, set apart from mass culture, standing in opposition to the powers that be. This means we must seriously address our relationship with technology.

While buying a bottle of water at the airport recently, I looked up to see a television program about mothers in Japan advocating for bringing back arranged marriages. They were complaining how their sons and daughters were so addicted to social media and video games they were emotionally and mentally stunted, unable to put down their phones long enough to properly date someone, let alone build a healthy marriage and raise children. The distressing population decline in Japan only proves these mothers' fears.

> Japan now has one of the lowest fertility rates in the world . . . By 2060, the government estimates, there will be just 87 million people in Japan; nearly half of them will be over 65. Without a dramatic change in either the birthrate or its restrictive immigration policies, Japan simply won't have enough workers to support its retirees, and will enter a demographic death spiral.[4]

One of the biggest questions we will face in the next fifty years is, What does it mean to be human in the age of technology? If the digital life promises us almost everything we want, why would we need other people? From virtual reality to artificial intelligence and the coming wave of human-like robot dolls for both sex and companionship, we are entering a brave new world as a species.

Sigmund Freud theorized that a human being's main source of motivation is to maximize pleasure and minimize pain. Austrian neurologist Victor Frankl argued an enhanced view, that life isn't about seeking pleasure as much as it is a quest for meaning. Frankl believed meaning rather than pleasure was the lifeblood of the human experience.

If you've taken an introductory psychology class, you may remember a pyramid displaying Abraham Maslow's *hierarchy of needs*. At the base of the pyramid are a human's most primal needs: oxygen, food, water, shelter, and sex. But those are the same as most mammals. The main difference between humans and animals is that animals have no existential ability. A dog never wonders *why* he's a dog or for *what* purpose. He just is what he is, motivated by his most primal desires.

Maslow believed that while human beings start at the base of the pyramid, our goal is to move to the very top, a place he called self-actualization. At the tip of the pyramid is what truly make us the flourishing creatures God intended. Maslow described the apex of the human experience as the need for morality, creativity, spontaneity, problem solving, lack of prejudice, self-esteem, confidence, achievement, and respect for others.

The perilous quest to the top of Maslow's pyramid is where human beings discover meaning and purpose. It is where we find the connection to the cosmos and a reason for living. But these needs are only satisfied in relation to others. Our journey for meaning is directly linked to other people, which is fundamental for human flourishing. Simply put, for our lives to have any purpose at all, we must find a noble quest and travel it alongside others. Only then can we move toward the true apex of the human experience.

Chapter 14

BOUND TOGETHER

*Struggling souls catch light from other souls
who are fully lit and willing to show it.*

———

CLARISSA PINKOLA ESTES

M any Amish teenagers count down the days until they
turn sixteen. After they are educated in the local Amish
school through eighth grade and grinding through manual
labor ever since, the rite of passage known as Rumspringa, or
"running around" as translated from the German, is the most
exciting time in an Amish teen's life. Rumspringa provides the
opportunity for Amish sixteen-year-olds to leave their families,
move out of the Amish community, and experience life in the
outside world for the first time.

With this newfound freedom, Amish teens will often move closer to cities and acquire more modern amenities—cars, mobile phones, and the latest fashions. Some of them, equipped with social media and the internet, do what many high school teens do when their parents aren't around: they throw epic parties. I'm not kidding. For two years and sometimes more, Amish teens in Pennsylvania, Ohio, Indiana, and Michigan host alcohol- and drug-filled ragers that would put any high school party to shame.

Indiana Sheriff Jeff Campos describes Amish parties, which often take place in rural and wooded areas, like this: "We'll find kids there from Illinois, from Ohio, from Michigan. All over. That's what makes these so big. Unfortunately when we do have to respond to a large gathering, party, and it's majority Amish, it's huge. Anywhere from 200–300 kids."[1]

In May of 2016, five Amish teenagers on Rumspringa were pulled over when Indiana state troopers caught them driving 110 miles per hour in a minivan and tossing cans of beer out the window. When the car was finally pulled over, officers found the seventeen-year-old driver had only a learner's permit and was accompanied by two other sixteen-year-old males, two sixteen-year-old girls, and additional cases of beer and whisky. The driver was charged with drunk driving, reckless endangerment, and littering. The other passengers faced underage drinking charges. State police eventually released the teens into the custody of relatives, although there was some difficulty locating the kids' parents because they don't use telephones.[2]

I first learned of Rumspringa from a documentary called *The Devil's Playground*, which quite aptly on the cover of the

DVD features an Amish girl wearing a bonnet, sitting in the back of a car, and lighting up a cigarette. The film also interviews non-Amish teenagers who expound passionately about the magnitude of Rumspringa gatherings. "Amish parties are the bomb!" screams one wide-eyed teenager.

While it seems chaotic on the outside, Rumspringa is a tradition that has a very distinct purpose in the Amish community. Amid the hangovers, new clothes, and smartphones, after two years of living in the outside world, Amish teens are given a choice. They can return to the community to be baptized as Amish, committing themselves forever, or they can stay in the "English" world, alienating themselves from their family and going about their life as they please. Remarkably, Amish baptism rates and reintegration *after* Rumspringa are nearly 90 percent. It's the single most effective mechanism to keeping the Amish tradition alive generation after generation. After two years of indulgence, they give up McDonald's for homegrown vegetables, fast cars for the horse and buggy, and electricity for the setting sun nine times out of ten. Teens return to the community not because they simply "got it out of their system," but because even as teenagers they recognize nothing is more important than their community. After the parties, clothes, and technology lose their shine, they realize what they value most are the connections with the people closest to them. Relationships matter.

A seventy-five-year study from Harvard concluded that people who were happiest at the end of their lives were the ones who maintained deep relationships with others.[3] Not only is pursuing human relationships the most effective way to boost your own levels of happiness, but it's also the most impactful thing you can do to change the world. I love the quote from Lilla Watson from the United Nations Decade For Women Conference: "If you have come here to help me, you are wasting your time. But if you have come because your liberation is bound up with mine, then let us work together."[4]

If you really want to change the world, whether it be across the globe or in your neighborhood, you must bind up your own liberation with those you are trying to help. This can only be done through the deep well of human relationships.

In the Rwandan refugee camps we work in, there are a handful of other organizations that provide medical care, food aid, and primary education. Repeatedly we've been told there is one key factor that sets These Numbers Have Faces apart from all the rest. Our refugee friends say we are the only people who physically come inside their homes, sit together to share a meal, laugh, and allow everyone to pray for each other. We'll bring visitors from across the world who report, time and time again, that this experience is the most powerful part of their entire trip. We've found the best delivery method for our work is simple: it's in the forging of friendships.

Never will I fully understand what it means to be a refugee, to flee a civil war, and to live for twenty years in a mud hut the size of my kitchen. But sitting on rickety benches in the dark eating Congolese food with our refugee friends is a small step toward binding up my liberation with that of others. The "white savior complex" is a real and dangerous threat to much of the good work around the world. But if it is based in friendship and done in the spirit of leveling social and economic hierarchies, experiences like this are where I've found God more than in any church service. It's in these moments that it's clear the only way to actually make change in the world is through the slow and methodical process of relationships.

One of our signature engagement tools at These Numbers Have Faces is an online platform called Impact Circles. Similar to the traditional child sponsorship model pioneered by organizations like World Vision and Compassion International, we personally connect individuals and groups around the globe with our university students in East Africa. Each student has an online dashboard where Impact Circle members can see photos and videos and track their academic and personal progress. But it also employs a messaging feature, facilitated by our Portland office, where sponsors can chat back and forth with the student they invest in.

We've seen amazing relationships forged through *Impact Circles*, with dozens of messages per week sent back and forth. For our students, the opportunity to have a champion in their corner is an amazing gift. And the *Impact Circle* members have a once-in-a-lifetime opportunity to invest in and connect with an African young person on a deep level. This is the power of technology used for good.

I believe deeply in the leveraging of technology to connect people around the globe to expand our empathy, solve problems, and build friendships. But we will also face a crisis as a species in the next fifty years because of it. I believe over the course of the next few decades, the deep investment in real human relationships will become a revolutionary act. People who embody deep character and use their gifts to invest in others will find themselves on the forefront of our moral history. This is where you want to be. Technology gives us access to others, but it's our character and commitment to humanity that will drive it forward. How you do this at our critical time in human history will define the type of person you are and will become.

Chapter 15

THE MOST REVOLUTIONARY
OF EMOTIONS

Could a greater miracle take place than
for us to look through each other's eye for
an instant?

———

HENRY DAVID THOREAU

Abraham Lincoln's early encounters with slavery would have happened as a child in rural Kentucky. In 1810, the number of slaves in Kentucky was small, about 8 percent of the population, and Lincoln's family was poor. They didn't run in the same circles with wealthy plantation owners, and with their strong Baptist beliefs, the family abhorred slavery. So much so that Lincoln's parents actually belonged to a small group of "kitchen-table abolitionists" who eventually encouraged them to leave Kentucky altogether for the northern states of Indiana and later Illinois.

At age nineteen, Lincoln and a friend were hired to man a flatboat down the Mississippi River from Illinois to the Gulf Coast to deliver cargo and goods to New Orleans. It was Lincoln's first trip into the heart of human slavery. Unloading cargo on the New Orleans city docks, Lincoln stumbled upon a slave auction and watched in horror as families were torn apart, beaten, pinched, inspected, dehumanized, and sold like livestock. Historians say it was this disturbing experience that brought the injustice and brutality of slavery into Lincoln's worldview, forever influencing his beliefs on the practice. As they pulled away from the New Orleans docks in 1831, Lincoln was quoted as saying, "By God, boys, let's get away from this. If ever I get a chance to hit that thing [slavery], I'll hit it hard."[1]

The trip back to Illinois provided even more trauma as seven escaped slaves attacked Lincoln's flatboat in an effort to steal the boat and make their way north. Lincoln, a skilled wrestler, and the crew were hurt in the melee but succeeded in fighting off the slaves and making it home safely to Illinois. It's interesting to visualize a lanky and sharp-knuckled teenager brawling with slaves he'd eventually set free.

Before Abraham Lincoln ever witnessed the injustice of the slave economy in New Orleans, he had experienced significant pain and suffering in his own life. Born in a one-room log cabin that was eighteen feet long with a dirt floor, Lincoln's early years were fraught with loss and poverty. His grandfather was shot in cold blood by a Native American in front of Abraham's father, Thomas, who would go on to physically abuse his son Abraham with regularity. Abe had a special and loving relationship with his mother, but at age nine, he helped his father construct a coffin and bury her after she died from "milk sickness," a fatal disease brought on by drinking milk from cows that had eaten certain forms of poisonous plants.

Whether in a log cabin in the nineteenth century or in an impoverished household in the present day, an early life of poverty and loss can transform the human heart into a charcoaled mass of bitterness. Yet for Lincoln, his experience as the abused son of a farmer actually made him more compassionate to the plight of others. Whether he knew it or not, his trip to New Orleans was his very first moment of obligation.

We can't know for sure what was going on in nineteen-year-old Abe's head that day on the docks of New Orleans. But given his past and his intimate knowledge of loss, shame, and abuse, we can speculate that he felt no small amount of empathy for those slaves. By definition, empathy is the identification and understanding of and engagement in the lives and well-being of others. It's not pity or sympathy but instead the "walking a mile in someone else's shoes" type of emotion. I believe if we can follow the empathic response of a lanky nineteen-year-old flatboat captain, we can build relationships with powerful consequences. For Abraham Lincoln, this is exactly what happened.

Empathy isn't only about feeling something significant when witnessing a gross injustice. Empathy is also the powerful emotion that enables you to connect with other people to solve problems. Decades after his flatboat experience, in the halls of political power, Lincoln became known for his skills in mediation and bipartisan negotiation. He was famous for his friendships with politicians on the opposite side of the aisle, and he cared deeply about the personal lives of his colleagues. He remembered their families' names and asked thoughtful questions, understanding their fears and concerns. It was from that baseline, one built upon relationships carefully cultivated, that he was able to create solutions to America's gravest challenges.

In a world dominated by power and money, traits of ambition and ruthlessness are celebrated. Empathy is seen as a "weak" emotion, an annoying characteristic of "feelers" employed by the likes of social workers, humanitarians, and drum-circle aficionados. Lincoln, a champion boxer and the son of an abusive farmer, was no kumbaya-singing idealist. Instead he used his empathic skills to bolster the pillars of his political leadership. His care for others made him a more strategic politician. Empathy made him strong, not weak.

Of course, the science backs this up. Empathy is considered by many psychologists to be essential to cooperation, problem solving, and human functioning in general. Researchers have described it as "social glue,"[2] binding people together, creating harmonious relationships, and enabling people who disagree to solve problems. While Lincoln's initial experience on the docks was the spark that lit the fire in his belly, it was his long-term empathic skills that created the advanced negotiations necessary to sign the Emancipation Proclamation in 1863, putting an end to American slavery.

Lincoln is the epitome of fulfilling a life of purpose and meaning. His work in orchestrating the destruction of a great injustice is one of the ultimate political and social accomplishments in American history. Although Lincoln is a once-in-a-generation leader, an advanced understanding of empathy is critical for success, no matter who you are. Empathy is an emotion that thrives in practical situations, functioning as a muscle that needs to be exercised, trained, and toned.

For those of us who are made for these times, the development of our empathic abilities is a top priority. Ordinary people who work their empathy muscles are capable of accomplishing extraordinary things. But it doesn't take a life-changing experience on the docks of New Orleans to start. The social glue of empathy is the extra care, a thoughtful question or compliment to someone whose life doesn't affect your own. It's the willingness to humanize those who disagree with you. Empathy is the greatest expression of our humanity.

Chapter 16

LIGHTHOUSE ON A HILL

*We draw people to Christ not by loudly
discrediting what they believe, by telling
them how wrong we are and how right we
are, but by showing them a light that is so
lovely that they want with all their hearts
to know the source of it.*

———

MADELEINE L'ENGLE

It was one of those days when everything sucked. Portland had hit freezing temperatures all week. I scraped ice off my windshield, trying to warm up with reheated, three-day-old coffee. The holiday season had barely begun and already I was hit with a tidal wave of work and stress. I was driving in my car, annoyed with everything and everyone. Anxiety, fear, fatigue, hunger. I'd slipped into that place where I just hated the person I was becoming more and more every minute.

At a stoplight ahead was a maroon Cadillac DeVille. I slowed up behind it, waiting for the light to turn. Green means go, but the Cadillac didn't move. I waited. I gave a light honk—maybe he was looking at his phone. Nothing. Then an elongated blast. I was seething. All my frustration cathartically poured into the blaring of the car horn.

The Cadillac door opened, and an elderly man stepped out onto the icy asphalt. His face was stern. *Oh crap.* I locked my doors, expecting an oncoming barrage of abuse for my tactless honking. Cars were lined up behind us as he shuffled up to my driver's side window. I cracked it an inch, just to be safe.

"Can you give me a push?" he asked. He was defeated, frustrated, and fatigued. Just like me.

"Um, ya, of course." I pulled the emergency brake and hopped out into the street. Putting my gloved hands on the back of his car, I looked back and saw the guy in the car behind me getting out. So did the guy behind him. As a team, we steered the broken-down Cadillac through the intersection and into a curbside parking spot. We all nodded to each other—guy stuff, playing it cool. The old man gave us all a wave of thanks and remarked that he had a tow truck on the way.

I got back in my car, and the light turned green. I drove through the intersection. I fiddled with the radio, and then it hit me—I felt better. Wow. And not just a little better, like all the way better. Instantly my stress, fear, and dread leveled off. It was a miracle, almost supernatural. How was this possible? Five minutes ago I hated everyone on earth. Then I pushed an old man's Cadillac DeVille thirty-five feet with three strangers, and suddenly I'm cured. Really?

As it turns out, the science on this phenomenon is quite robust. Social connections, like the one I had with the Cadillac, that engage the physicality of our bodies and the empathic centers of our brains, release the reserves of a chemical called oxytocin. On a macro level, oxytocin is the chemical that helps us bond with others and handle stress. It's most famously known as the chemical released during sex, but it also helps mothers bond with their children, reduces social anxiety, relieves pain, fights depression, and even promotes generosity. I'm not a doctor, therapist, or psychologist, but exercising your empathy muscles will make you feel better. Honestly.

Studies show that volunteering can boost happiness, decrease depression, relieve stress, and help you live longer. The same is true for charitable giving. In 1989, economist James Andreoni theorized the *Warm-Glow Giving* phenomenon, concluding that people received positive emotional feelings activated by helping others. On average, people who gave away more of their money reported significantly higher levels of happiness than those who didn't.

In 2016, one in every six Americans had filled a prescription for antidepressants.[1] I'm not against antidepressants—I'm currently on them. But supplementing pharmaceuticals with the deep well of human relationships and concrete acts of service, empathy, and exercise is the sure-fire way to feel better.

———

On May 20, 2012, eighteen-year-old Takunda Mavima was

driving home from a party when he lost control and crashed his car into an off-ramp near Grand Rapids, Michigan. Riding in the car were seventeen-year-old Tim See and fifteen-year-old Krysta Howell. Both were killed in the accident. Takunda Mavima lived.

Mavima pleaded guilty to all charges and was sentenced to between thirty months and fifteen years in prison. Despite their unimaginable grief and anger, both the sister and the father of the victim, Tim See Sr., gave a moving address to the court on behalf of Mavima, urging the judge to give him a light sentence. "I am begging you to let Takunda Mavima make something of himself in the real world—don't send him to prison and get hard and bitter, that boy has learned his lesson a thousand times over and he'll never make the same mistake again."[2]

When the hearing ended, the victim's family made their way across the courtroom to embrace, console, and publicly forgive Mavima. I'm reminded of the quote commonly attributed to Fred Rogers, "The only thing evil can't stand is forgiveness."

Conventional wisdom of the justice system says we should blame this teenager for taking a life and banish him to prison, believing his suffering will ease the suffering of the victim's families. An eye for an eye. I don't know the See family in Michigan, but I can suspect something remarkable of their character as a family. On that fateful day in a Grand Rapids courtroom, I believe the empathic and reconciliatory response from the See family was no accident. They didn't wake up the day of the trial and just determine in that moment to forgive Takunda Mavima like they did. This family of faith had built layers upon layers of small, empathic acts leading up to this defining moment. Forgiving the man who killed your son is probably the hardest thing Tim See Sr. and his family have ever done. But I bet they've had years of practice.

Character is built by small virtues over time, even the ones we don't realize we are exercising. A friendly hello here, a word of encouragement there. My mom used to say that people with good character are the ones who always return their shopping carts, because they understand a nineteen-year-old making seven dollars an hour will have to fish it out of a nearby planter when you're too lazy to walk twenty feet.

In his book *The Social Animal*, David Brooks writes that these seemingly insignificant actions of virtue are so powerful, we can actually rewire our brains for long-term empathy and compassion through them. These small acts then have the ability to layer on top of each other over time, so when the massive opportunity arises, it's far easier to respond with grace in action.

When I helped the old man push his Cadillac in the snow, I instantly felt better. But it also layered an act of service that could have been the jumping-off point for another one down the road. Don't get me wrong, we aren't saved by our good works. But neither are we saved without them. The question is, Are we open to scanning for these empathic moments in our daily lives and using them as stepping-stones to something bigger and better?

In Luke 16, Jesus tells the parable of the shrewd manager. He says, "Whoever can be trusted with very little can also be trusted with much, and whoever is dishonest with very little will also be dishonest with much" (v. 10). I believe the same truth applies for our actions of empathy and character. If we can be trusted to respond with empathy in the small ways, we'll be given the opportunity to respond in the big ones.

The See family will never have their son back. But in the swelling sea of human destruction, the little story of Takunda Mavima and a family from Michigan is a lighthouse on a hill, a beacon of hope guiding the way for all our ships to pass through.

Chapter 17

GUERNICA

Abraham Lincoln, Mother Teresa, Mahatma Gandhi—they all seem a cut above the rest. Their compassion, empathy, and ability to mobilize for good were otherworldly. When we compare ourselves to the heroes of our history, the chasm between the everyday person to one of these larger-than-life figures seems so wide, why even try to make the leap? Then you meet people like Daryl Davis, Sarah Thebarge, the See family, and the people of Le Chambon. As I hope you have seen, they were ordinary, just like you and me. Their stories should inspire us to believe it is possible to be made for these times and to do something about it. Even better, we have science on our side too.

In his fascinating book, *The Empathic Civilization*, economist Jeremy Rifkin argues that human beings are actually "soft wired" to biochemically empathize with the plight of others, the first step toward solving the world's greatest challenges.[1] In making this claim, Rifkin questions the individualistic and selfish nature of the human narrative as a whole, claiming it is science, not philosophy, that should be our guiding principle for understanding human nature.

Stay with me here.

In the 1990s, scientists in Parma, Italy, hooked a primate up to an MRI bran scan machine and gave it the task of cracking nuts and eating them. Scientists could then track which neurons lit up on the monkey's brain while it engaged in simple problem solving. During the experiment, in a bizarre happenstance, an oblivious and hungry scientist wandered into the lab and came upon the bowl of nuts. Cracking one open, he ate it in front of the monkey, and much to everyone's surprise, the MRI lit up. The exact same neurons had fired while watching the human eat the nut as when the monkey ate the nuts himself.

Initially, the scientists thought the MRI machine was broken and needed to be repaired. But after additional tests and experimentation with other primates, including chimpanzees and their large, human-like neocortices, scientists concluded that humans, primates, and perhaps dolphins and canines have what are called "mirror neurons." These mirror neurons allow us to witness an event happen to someone else and actually identify with that person as if we are experiencing it ourselves. Even if the event is something we haven't actually experienced, our mirror neurons have the biogenetic ability to produce small emotions that feel strikingly original.

Now we don't need science to tell us that when we witness a vat of snakes poured on a gameshow contestant, it's some neurological miracle when we get the heebie-jeebies as well. After watching a video of a child's follow-through with a baseball bat directly into his father's groin, most male viewers can swear they legitimately felt something powerful tingling in their own midsection. But beyond the physical, with spinoffs from the initial research in Italy, scientists can now prove that mirror reactions take place for a range of emotions as well, such as anger, rejection, joy, excitement, despair, and many more.

What's fascinating is that the responses to the plights of others aren't just true in adults. Apparently you don't need matured cerebral function to empathize with others, as children understand empathy quite early, even when it's only in their subconscious. Anyone who has ever worked in a hospital, nursery, or daycare can attest that when one baby cries, almost miraculously, other babies begin to do the same. Even though the second, third, fourth, and (for the love of God) fifth and sixth babies aren't experiencing the same discomfort the initial baby is feeling, the other babies are biochemically softwired to experience, in some way, the plight of baby number one.

Early Enlightenment philosophers like John Locke and Adam Smith would insist that humans are naturally individualistic, materialistic, utilitarian, and pleasure seeking. From a "religious" perspective, and on the grounds of original sin, I understand and sympathize with that view. But I can't say I'm not intrigued when modern science on empathy concludes that humans are softwired and biogenetically built to "experience another's plights as if we are experiencing them ourselves." Rifkin's optimism is seductive. He goes on to refer to the human race as *homo empathicus*, and in contrast to the Enlightenment thinkers, he concludes that we are created not for violence, aggression, and self-interest but rather for sociability, attachment, affection, and companionship. Along with those virtues, it is the drive for "belonging" that is most pronounced. Perhaps it is that innate desire for belonging, affection, and companionship that drives humans toward materialism, violence, individualism, and pleasure in the first place.

———

One of my favorite paintings is Pablo Picasso's haunting *Guernica*. An abstract piece depicting the Nazi bombing of Guernica, a Basque country village in northern Spain, Picasso's piece became a cultural symbol denouncing the horrors of war. I used to enjoy *Guernica* from a state of melancholy, fixating on a postcard of it when I felt the slight tinge of depression. I would stare at *Guernica* to feel sad on purpose, put on *Jimmy Eat World*, and just soak in the pain. It hurt, but it hurt so good. I enjoyed the darkness of *Guernica* as a privileged outsider from middle-class America, never considering what it would actually be like to be one of the black and white bodies twisted and contorted in death.

While Guernica always felt a million miles away, in 2014, I swallowed a sliver of the metallic taste of war when I spent a late night with a twenty-year-old Congolese refugee named Phillip. A brilliant young man, Phillip is thin, handsome, and all smiles when you speak about the thing he loves most, Liverpool Football Club.

Over dinner at a hotel in Rwanda, talking about soccer grew into learning about Phillip's life. How his family fled the Congo when the Rwandan genocide spilled into his village. How the refugee camp they settled in wasn't secure enough to keep the militias out. How he watched his family murdered in front of him. How he was thrown into a burning hut. How the scars are still visible on his face. We talked about that for a little while. Then we talked about soccer again, about how his accounting classes were going, and about how he just downloaded some new songs on his phone. Phillip has been through a horror impossible to describe. But today, he's just a college kid in the These Numbers Have Faces university program. He dresses sharp and chats up cute girls at his school. He studies hard and watches movies with his friends on the weekends.

Guy Davenport once wrote, "Distance negates responsibility."[2] Years ago, this may have been true. But in our globalized world, no matter the distance, we not only have an ability to connect but also, I would argue, a responsibility.

Philosopher Martin Buber is best known for his theory of I-Thou and I-It relationships. Buber concludes that when living in a one-dimensional way, humans create "I-It" relationships to merely serve their own purposes. The local plumber is just a phone call and a labor mechanism to fix your toilet, a basic business transaction of supply and demand. An "I-Thou" relationship, on the other hand, is when your plumber has a name, has kids who attend the school down the street, and is someone with interests and dreams like you.

As I sat there with Phillip on a warm Rwandan night, I remember thinking, *If only people had the opportunity to know him like I do.* If only they would meet him and empathize, they'd see Africa differently, they'd see war differently, and they'd question their priorities. They'd realize there may be more to life then attaining the comforts of the American dream. After the flat-screen TV and the two-car garage, now what?

Abraham Lincoln was a man of impressive faith and conviction: humble beginnings, strong character, a talented politician with all the skills to be a great president. But I wonder if he'd be remembered today as the man who brought down slavery had he not taken that trip down the Mississippi River at nineteen years old. His experience on the New Orleans docks was pivotal in shaping his character. Had he not witnessed the slave auction, empathized with the people he saw, fought off the seven slaves with his bare hands as they stormed his flatboat, would Lincoln have been the man who ended slavery thirty-two years later?

When we allow them to, empathy-driven "I-Thou" relationships radically change us. In my years as a social entrepreneur and doing research on some of the greatest leaders of all time, one thread remains constant. Relationships are the instigators of the most sincere and powerful moments of obligation. Our empathic response to the plight of others is the linchpin that will define our lives.

THIS IS WHERE

the rubber

HITS

the

ROAD...

Part V | THE MOMENTUM

It's building now . . .

You've fought back against The Resistance, bitten off a mouthful of grit, prioritized relationships, and gathered good people around you. Results begin to fall your way. People want what you're selling. You're energized. That pinging sound in the distance, the pinpoint of your meaning and purpose—it feels closer and closer. God is up to something in you; you're feeling it now. The momentum is gaining.

But if you're not careful, it is in this place that you could make a grave mistake. You're tempted to put all you have into the mining cart called momentum and ride it solo into unknown depths. You must resist this adventure.

At times I've let my own momentum spiral out of control. Thinking I could simply do it all, I've put myself ahead of the God who brought me here and neglected the ones closest to me in the pursuit of purpose. When spiritual and physical health are in danger, nervous breakdowns come next—or worse.

The following chapters aim to prioritize what matters most. We'll discover the art of balancing *The Active Tension*, place God at the center of our pursuits, and reconsider what success truly means.

Momentum is good. But learning to put the brakes on it is even better.

Chapter 18

YOU CAN'T BUILD THE KINGDOM WITHOUT THE KING

Christ is always with us, always asking for room in our hearts.

———

DOROTHY DAY

Harvey and Lois Seifert wrote a tiny book called *Liberation of Life*, much of it devoted to the idea of finding the balance between loving God and loving our neighbor. They describe this balance as a bird soaring on the wings of spiritual devotion and social action simultaneously.

An ancient saying suggested that there are two wings by which we rise, one being personal piety and the other community charity. No one can fly by flapping only one wing. It is impossible to be sincere in our worship of God without expecting to do the will of God. It is equally impossible to do the full will of God without the guidance and empowerment of a vital personal relationship with God.[1]

If we're to find the ecstatic heights of devotional life, it can only be achieved by acting for the pragmatic benefit of others. If we're to join God to work for the least of these, it can only be sustained through the careful diligence of faith and personal piety. Discovering this delicate balance is the ultimate goal.

While living in Belfast in my early twenties, trying to find social and spiritual balance resulted in one of the most profound spiritual experiences of my life. God had been particularly silent, and I was quite lonely at the time when I signed up for an intercessory prayer session with a local pastor at a nearby Presbyterian church. Pastor Derek was recommended by a friend as someone who could perhaps give me some insight into my direction in life, my "calling," and how to find God in dark times. To be honest, I'm not really the type to volunteer myself for these types of meetings. Whether it's pride or awkwardness or both, the thought of a stranger telling me what to do with my life makes my defenses go up. But God has a funny way of moving in the world, and oftentimes the most uncomfortable path is the exact one to choose.

I met Pastor Derek in his office. He was like a grandfather figure, wonderfully kind, and I felt comfortable immediately. I sat on a couch, and he pulled up a chair next to me and asked if he could put his hand over my heart. This is where it started to get weird. Derek sat in silence for a moment, asked God to speak to me through him, and then blew the roof off the place. He whispered,

> Justin, I see you walking into a big room, and you're carrying all these boxes. You have them stacked on top of each other, a few balancing in each hand, and labeled on each box are different phrases like community, social justice, hope, and compassion. And Jesus is there, and he's standing in front of you with a big smile on his face.
>
> Justin, Jesus wants me to tell you that he is so very proud of you. You are carrying the things he cares most about, the things that are closest to his heart, but for right now, he needs you to put down those boxes so he can give you a hug.

By this time I'm leaning my head back on the couch as tears roll down my cheeks. It was all so piercingly accurate, exactly what I wanted and didn't want to hear at the same time. I'd never met Derek before, and he knew nothing about me or what I was even doing in Northern Ireland. Yet this was the most true and honest thing anyone had ever said to me. It was from God.

Derek's words struck right in the pit of my soul and had me reflecting on all the times I had been working *for* God but not actually *with* God—the times I had done things in his name but never actually invited him into it. I had been putting so much pressure on myself to complete God's work that I had begun to neglect God in the process. The work had become an idol. Even worse, I was embarrassed for all the times I had prayed for God to bless the things I was up to but didn't stop to simply ask if I could join in what he was already doing.

As Henri Nouwen writes, "The way of Jesus can only be walked with Jesus. If I want to do it alone, it becomes a form of inverse heroism as fickle as heroism itself."[2]

Derek got up while I sniffled a bit more on the couch and blew my nose into the sleeve of my sweatshirt. He checked email on his office computer while I sat and stared out the window. A few minutes passed, and then it was over. I got up and shook his hand. Derek winked affectionately, and I walked out into the blustery Belfast street. I never saw him again.

Learning how to find social and spiritual balance has been one of the greatest challenges of my adult life. In moments of pain and uncertainty, my relationship with Christ becomes paramount, prioritized above the rest. But in times of ease and rest, it's remarkable how quickly it can fade away. I'm sure you can attest to this struggle as well. One secret I've found is embodying a spirit of gratefulness in all things. If I'm attending a graduation ceremony for our university graduates in East Africa, I give thanks that it's God's doing, not mine. And when I'm pinned to the bed in agony, with fear and anxiety ripping at my chest, I'm grateful God has given me the opportunity to work alongside him despite the pain.

While describing the spiritual battles in building These Numbers Have Faces, my friend Sam once said to me, "You can't build the kingdom without the King." How right he is. As it says in the Psalms, unless the Lord builds the house, the workers labor in vain. Searching the depths of our spiritual lives reveals all the darkness we've tried to hide, but it's the only way to answer the invitation to join in God's redemption of humanity.

As much as we may try to deny it, we humans are God's secret weapon. We're the least credible allies, woefully unprepared and prone to fear, desertion, and trite insecurities. But God chooses us anyway. If God were to perform a cost-benefit analysis, he'd see the human population as a huge liability. But logic would be counterintuitive to the revolutionary and tactical dynamic of the kingdom itself. God invites us to work alongside him to reveal heaven on earth. In our obedience and partnership with Christ, we become human change agents, rescuing both creation and others, all the while being rescued ourselves. We save lives, all the while being saved. For God to just do it on his own would actually defeat the whole purpose.

Like my experience with Pastor Derek in Belfast, finding the successful balance between competing beliefs or actions is a profound way of living I call The Active Tension. The Active Tension is the sacred balance of all things, big and small. It's social and spiritual, professional and personal, public and private. Those living well in The Active Tension create a preemptive plan to manage the tension of work with the responsibilities of home. They know when it is time to rest and when it is time to work. Those in The Active Tension hold equally the call for a deep spiritual life and the righteous indignation against injustice. They treat the CEO of Starbucks and the green-aproned barista with the same respect and dignity. In the following chapters we'll explore what it means to live in The Active Tension in a way I believe can become the foundation for a life of meaning and purpose during this unique time in history.

Chapter 19

THE RAINBOW NATION

*People may spend their whole lives
climbing the ladder of success only to
find, once they reach the top, that the
ladder is leaning against the wrong wall.*

THOMAS MERTON

The spirit of Nelson Mandela is alive and well in the These Numbers Have Faces office in Portland. Direct from Cape Town, a large, framed tapestry of his image is hung prominently next to my desk. To describe Mandela as a hero of mine would be a gross understatement. Rising from the depths of poverty to a law degree in a country where black South Africans were barred from the country's best universities, Mandela breathed life into the rumblings of revolution.

Imprisoned for twenty-seven years in Robben Island Prison for anti-apartheid activity, he became an inspirational educator to countless inmates; his tutelage was a beacon of hope in one of the most hopeless places imaginable. So relentless was his passion for education, inmates began referring to the island as "Nelson Mandela University," a far cry from the countless stories of psychological destruction that had made the prison famous.

Despite his early history with political violence, from the tiny barred window in a six-foot-square cell, Mandela conceived the peaceful vision of a post-apartheid South Africa: a society not of black and white, but a rainbow nation of vigor and opportunity founded on common principles of mutual respect and dignity. He built relationships with white prison guards, spoke to them in their native Afrikaans, and became a staunch advocate for reconciliation as the ultimate cure to South Africa's racial divide. Mandela believed that people and the positions they hold can change, a notion conceived within the transformation of his own human heart.

His vision for a truly democratic South Africa laid the foundation for the country's first ever multi-racial elections in 1994. First-time voters braved lines miles long, and they sang and danced all the way to the polls. Mandela was elected president, apartheid laws were dismantled, and South Africa became the new hope for a post-colonial Africa.

Some early evenings after our staff has gone home, it's just Nelson and me in our office. I'll kick off my shoes, crank the punk rock anthems of my youth, and let the nostalgia of simpler times sink in. Yet when I look up at the wall to his coffee-toned skin and those deep, flickering eyes, I sense him urging me to protect the ones closest to me.

As *Time* magazine selects another "Person of the Year" to delight in, I can't help but notice that our global icons are most often acclaimed for the great accomplishments in their public lives rather than scrutinized for the great failings in their personal ones. This surely isn't true with everyone, but some of the greatest heroes of modern history were problematic family men.

The personal history of Mandela is often muted by his magnificence. The T-shirts and trinkets imprinted with his face don't tell the story of his six children who never knew him. His family braved decades of fear for the life of their father, their hearts stopping with sinking dread each time the telephone rang. Of his three marriages, the most public was to controversial political activist Winnie Madikizela Mandela. Much of their relationship was spent with Mandela behind bars. Rumors of her infidelity drove them apart, as did her suspected involvement in politically motivated human rights abuses that continue to call her name into question.

Mandela's eldest son, Thembi, was killed in a car crash in 1969. Imprisoned on Robben Island at the time, Mandela wasn't permitted to attend his son's funeral. He wept on the floor of a dusty cell, locked in by metal and sorrow. Longtime friend and fellow prisoner Walter Sislu held his hand for hours, the only human contact that could connect him to his grieving family.

Selections of Mandela's stunning autobiography, *Long Walk to Freedom*, were buried in the garden on Robben Island to avoid detection. It remains to this day one of the most critically acclaimed political autobiographies of all time. In it, Mandela writes of the fateful day he learned of his son's death:

I thought back to one afternoon when Thembi was a boy and he came to visit me at a safe house in Cyrildene that I used for secret ANC work. Between my underground political work and legal cases, I had not been able to see him for some time. I surprised him at the house and found him wearing an old jacket of mine that came to his knees. He must have taken some comfort and pride in wearing his father's clothing, just as I once did with my own father's. When I had to say goodbye again, he stood up tall, as if he were already grown, and said, "I will look after the family while you are gone."[1]

As endearing as Thembi is in this role of "man of the house," it is equally heartbreaking. He's playing adult in an oversized jacket of an absent father who has chosen a political cause over his family. I don't mean to be overly critical of Mandela. He is an awe-inspiring leader, made by God for his unique time in history. But despite heeding his call and embracing his destiny as the godfather of South Africa, he suffered a secondary tension of how to balance his calling and his family in both hands.

Arguably the most consistent hardship I hear is people like me struggling with whether it's truly possible to do meaningful work while also being actively engaged as a spouse and parent. I've heard story after story, many of them gut wrenching, of this tension between work and family. More often than not, families are the ones who suffer.

Even more challenging are people wired for the social good. There are so many examples of magnetic leaders up to their eyeballs in meaning and purpose—inspiring others, caring for the poorest among us—while at home their own children resent them. A colleague of mine has committed the bulk of his professional life to serving displaced people in war-torn regions. Once he came home from a trip to South Sudan only to have his five-year-old daughter ask, "Daddy, do you love children in Africa more than you love me?" Heartbreak.

I attended a conference in New York and heard an inspiring talk from a successful Wall Street CEO. He emboldened us with his tales of risk taking and innovation. New products were launched in days and sold for hundreds of millions of dollars. He jetsetted around the world, meeting foreign dignitaries and turning the financial sector on its head, all the while giving away massive amounts of money to charitable organizations. It was a story of success everyone in the room had dreamed about.

Then came the hammer. In his pursuit of global innovation, success, and next-level generosity, everything at home had completely fallen apart. His wife had left him, and his teenage children were estranged. He found himself a broken mess, slumped at the kitchen table of a six-bedroom house he now occupied alone.

Most people don't realize the damage they are doing until it's too late, as if the gifts for our kids when we return home from a long trip really make up for being gone in the first place. As I've learned in my own life, the sacred balance of family and work is the ultimate quagmire of The Active Tension, one I know will plague me for most of my adult life. The only solution I can think to enact is to recognize the tension, admit I have a problem, and do small things daily to make up for lost time.

Chapter 20

PUT YOUR HOUSE IN ORDER

In 1965, a man named Ray Davey and a diverse mix of friends founded the Corrymeela Community on the north coast of Northern Ireland. The timing of the community's inception was prescient as the early 1970s saw surges of violence and trauma from the violent conflict in Northern Ireland. Like nothing of its kind at the time, Corrymeela provided a safe and open space for dialogue and reconciliation for many of the victims and perpetrators involved in the Northern Ireland conflict. Nearly half a century later, Davey is a hero among many in the province for his tireless work in conflict resolution and peacebuilding.

There is a rumor that at an early point in their work, Corrymeela was hosting a big peacebuilding seminar where a woman raised her hand and asked very pointedly, "What can I do to bring about peace in my country? What can I do specifically to work for reconciliation?"

Rather than promoting the work of Corrymeela or speaking

about broad topics of global justice, Davey looked directly at the woman and asked, *"You want to be a peacebuilder?"*

The woman nodded.

"You want to change the world?"

She nodded again.

"Here's the secret. Go home and put your house in order."

Hearing this story was an arrow-through-the-heart moment for me. It unearthed my greatest fear of all. I'm not scared of failure; I'm scared of success that blinds me to the most important priorities, the responsibilities in my own household: my wife, children, and relationships—with God and with others.

My dad, Steve, used to take two afternoons off a week to play soccer with me in our backyard when I was growing up. At the time, I didn't know any different. Only now as a father and entrepreneur do I understand just how radical this time investment truly was. For my dad, the investment in my brother, Ryan, and me was his personal mission, one worth far more than his career. Could he have made more money and been more successful? Absolutely. But he sacrificed his own professional ambition for me. My dad believed that the greatest change he could make in the world was to build in his sons the self-confidence to lead as character-driven men of God.

My mother, Janice, is my inspiration for the world of ideas, theology, politics, and social action. When I was a baby, she prayed over me in my crib that I would grow up to become a man who would impact the world. She hilariously trained me, at age three, to learn the presidents and prime ministers of the world, with my dad adding a Pavlovian bell to aid in the memorization.

"Justin, who is the prime minister of England?"

"Margaret Thatcher!" *Ding!*

"Who is the president of the United States?"

"Ronald Reagan!" *Ding!*

"Who is the dictator of Chile?"

"General Pinochet!" *Ding!*

At our Friday night dinners growing up, my mom would break out both the *Los Angeles Times* and our local newspaper (both of which she'd already read cover to cover) and do a current events session with the whole family. In her mind, even if I was only in seventh grade, it was important I knew what was happening in Washington, DC, the Middle East, and Latin America. At the time, both my brother and I despised these sessions. Looking back on it, her investment in cultivating a world beyond the borders of my own mind has shaped me in unimaginable ways.

The sacrifice and investment both my parents made in me has set the bar for how I want to live my life as a husband, father, and entrepreneur. It also represents the largest stumbling block to successfully navigating The Active Tension. I believe I've been uniquely called by God to grow enterprises and share ideas that impact people. I'm pretty sure that's my thing. The privilege of a middle-class upbringing, the hundreds of thousands of frequent flyer miles, and extra pages added to my passport only highlight the opportunities I've had to do this around the world. But it also means I've missed out on some critical milestones as a father. When my daughter was very young, she'd forget who I was while I was in Africa and cry when I'd try to hold her. On the days when my mind is churning and the stress is building, I might physically be at home, but with eyes glazed over, I'm not mentally there. In these moments I'm betraying the lessons my father taught me.

You may have heard the age-old question, "How do children spell love?" The answer: t-i-m-e. I've often reflected on that period of my life as a child with my dad in the backyard, the bulk of which, truthfully, I don't even remember too well. Writing this book actually gave me the opportunity to dig deeper with my dad, to get to the root of his sacrifice. For my father, his motivation for taking time off work to be with me actually came from three unique places. First, it came from challenges with his own father. Many men in the post-Depression era didn't employ the personal and cultural abilities necessary to build emotional intimacy with their children. This was the era when fathers shook the hands of their sons and withheld the highly sought after "I'm proud of you, son" for only the most important moments.

My grandfather was a successful orthodontist in Sacramento, California, and like all of us, a byproduct of his culture. He wasn't an emotionally cold or distant father. He just assumed it was his wife's role to dole out affection accordingly. Much of this is due to the fact that at age five, my grandfather lost his own father (my great-grandfather) to a railroad accident in the deserts of Nevada. My grandfather ended up alone on the streets of San Francisco and never actually internalized a model for what parenting looks like.

Second, my father was deeply influenced by my mom's father, Harry Johnson. Somewhat countercultural for his day, my grandfather on my mother's side showed great affection, silliness, and love for his children in a way my own father had never seen modeled before. Harry became a mentor to my dad and taught him the ways of both working hard in a career while being ever-present emotionally with his wife and family. Harry skillfully balanced The Active Tension.

The final piece of the foundation for my father's investment in me was his vocation as a marriage and family therapist. He was fascinated by psychology and through his study and eventual profession saw the all-too-obvious correlation between broken adults and broken childhoods. The statement that always opened the floodgates with his most tumultuous clients was simple: "Tell me about your childhood."

It was these three experiences that shaped my father into the parent he became, and he in turn shaped me. My dad recalled a tangible moment when I was only a few years old when he stopped and said to himself out loud, "One of my goals in life is to have a deeply significant emotional relationship with my children. This will be equally or more important than my financial success."

We often hear about the "sins of the father" being passed down through the generations. I believe this happens more often than we like to think. But gifts of the father can be passed down as well. My father's courage to break the mold in his parenting has created a ripple effect that he could never have envisioned. It has made waves not only in my family life but in my professional life as well. The relationship-driven and people-centered DNA of These Numbers Have Faces is a direct result of my parents' investment in me. Thousands of young people have been inspired by their example that I've simply passed on almost innately.

Being made for these times means you employ the long game. We act not just for today but for the generations who will come after us. I believe those who can balance The Active Tension are the ones who truly shape the future. They may never see the end results, but by upholding their commitments today, they lay the groundwork for tomorrow.

Like most things, The Active Tension is impossible to navigate alone. The delicate nature of social and spiritual balance takes heavenly discipline. Walking the tightrope between career and family demands spiritual fortitude. To give 100 percent to all of life's demands is physically impossible. Trying to do so will send us careening off a cliff. And it's in times of intense stress when The Resistance mounts its next plan of attack. But we have a chance when we employ the power of Christ, when we lay out our troubles with The Active Tension and ask earnestly for help in balancing them. Without God, The Active Tension simply devolves into stress. But with God, it is our steady hand through the fog.

Chapter 21

ENOUGH

If you can't feed a hundred people, feed just one.

───────

MOTHER TERESA

I was eleven years old when the film *Schindler's List* was released. I remember we had a babysitter the night my parents went to see it in the theatre, and my mom came home overwhelmed with grief, her eyes glazed over. It wasn't until years later, after a trip to *Blockbuster* to pick up the blue and yellow VHS tape, that I sat on the floor of my living room and watched it for the first time. It's a brilliant film, but the monstrosity of evil, even in black and white, is so gruesome that I can't imagine seeing it again. While I've forgotten most of it, one of the final scenes has never left me.

Oskar Schindler, played by Liam Neeson, was a German industrialist and a wealthy man. Using his successful company as a front for Resistance activities, Schindler is dressed in a suit, standing in front of the 1,100 Jews he has secretly employed in his factory to avoid Nazi detection. He has just learned that the war has finally ended, meaning the 1,100 Jewish workers are now safe. The daily, paralyzing fear of their discovery is over, and they won't be sent to Nazi concentration camps. They are free.

Surrounded by all the workers, Schindler's Jewish accountant Itzhak Stern, played by Ben Kingsley, walks up to Schindler and hands him a ring. Stern explains the inscription: *"It's Hebrew, from the Talmud. It says whoever saves one life saves the world entire."*

Shaking, Schindler fumbles with the ring, accidently dropping it on the ground. He retrieves it, sliding it onto his finger, and grasps the hand of his old friend Stern. Pulling him close, Schindler whispers, *"I could have got more out. I could have got more."*

Stern replies, *"There are 1,100 people who are alive because of you."*

From there, Schindler spirals into guilt and disbelief.

"If I had made more money. I could have done more. I threw away so much money."

He points at his car. *"Why did I keep this car? That's ten people right there."* Grasping at his gold lapel pin on his jacket, he breaks down in tears, sobbing, *"This pin, it's gold. I could have got one more person, but I didn't. I didn't."*

Oskar Schindler was a man made for a specific time in history, but despite his heroics, he is overcome with guilt.

Schindler can't help but recognize how simple sacrifices of irrelevant material goods could have saved dozens more. In this moment, he is burdened by his own success, battling the perils of a stunning achievement with the most precious gift of all: real human lives.

You may not be Oskar Schindler, but we all face the same struggle today, no matter what we do. When is enough, enough? When can we honestly say that we have succeeded? Is it the numbers in a bank account, a child going off to college, a golf-laden retirement dream? Maybe it's saving the lives of 1,100 people. But what if the goal is 1,101? Is saving 1,100 still a success?

Measuring and defining success is something I've struggled with deeply in my work at These Numbers Have Faces. Is the answer purely data driven? When we graduate ten thousand college students and invest in one thousand entrepreneurs, will it be considered a win? Or is it an achievement metric? Maybe when one of our graduates becomes a member of parliament or starts a big tech company, then we can be satisfied. Maybe it's when we have a $10 million-dollar budget or employ one hundred staff. Perhaps it's when we've fully achieved our mission and can actually cease to exist. Will I be happy then?

———

One of our graduates from Rwanda is a young man named Kamali. His story is like other stories you've read in this book; he was born in a refugee camp, got great grades, but because of his refugee status was unable to receive funding for university. After joining our leadership program, he graduated with a degree in finance right when we began piloting an innovative program that would bring our very best graduates from East Africa to the United States for summer internships with some of our favorite corporate partners.

Unemployment for young people is high in East Africa. While our students are exceptionally talented, we speculated an American internship at the top of their résumé could give our graduates an extra edge when they returned home seeking employment. Kamali was a standout in our program and upon graduation was selected by an American CPA firm, Delap, to join them as a summer intern in Portland.

However, securing a visa and passport for Kamali proved to be more challenging than we imagined. Kamali is Congolese, but he had been living in Rwanda since he was three years old. His mother, Elizabeth, carried Kamali on her back when they fled the Democratic Republic of Congo after the Rwandan genocide. His refugee status made him ineligible for a Rwandan passport, and as part of the persecuted Congolese Tutsi ethnic group, it was also extremely dangerous for him to travel back to the Congo to secure a passport. Kamali had never returned to Congo since he left at the height of the civil war in 1997, but he knew an internship in America could be a game changer for him and his family. So he decided to risk it.

Working with friends and an embassy contact, Kamali crossed the border into Goma, a large city in the Eastern Congo. Careful to hide his Rwandan accent and blend in at all costs, Kamali literally risked his life for a three-month internship for a CPA firm in Portland. Six weeks later, a package with his new passport arrived at our office in Rwanda. Kamali beamed and held it close to his chest.

He arrived at the Portland airport to cheers and hand-drawn

signs from our team. Along with the other interns that first summer, we couldn't believe they were actually here. As we knew he would, Kamali worked extremely hard and had an incredible internship experience with Delap. He even got to spend a few weeks working in the finance office of the Portland Timbers soccer team.

Alongside the knowledge he gained, Kamali made a decent salary while in Portland and was able to pay back his loan to These Numbers Have Faces in full, which supported a new first-year student in the program. Returning home to Rwanda with a stronger résumé and a powerful new experience under his belt, our assumptions about employment turned out to be true. Kamali had risen to the top of the pack during job interviews and was quickly selected to work for a local CPA firm in Kigali, Rwanda, as an auditor.

With no plans of moving, Kamali's parents and family were still living in the refugee camp surviving off the pittance of a monthly stipend from the United Nations. But Kamali's new job meant that he made over seven times the income of his parents. His skillset, determination, and salary made it possible for Kamali to send his younger siblings to better schools and ensure his family ate three meals per day, something they hadn't done in decades.

I'll never forget the day Kamali texted me to say he'd gotten the job at the CPA firm in Rwanda. A momentous wave of peace rushed over me. It was the culmination of years of hard work for our team in building a program for refugees, securing funding, providing leadership training, and piloting the summer internship. Not to mention the personal risk Kamali took to secure his passport and visa.

The peace I felt from Kamali's job announcement was the realization that his success was enough for me. Meeting benchmarks and growing budgets had never fulfilled me. But with that one phone call, I was done scrambling to reach the top of some mountain that only grew taller and taller with each step. We'd had countless achievements from other graduates and entrepreneurs, but there was something about Kamali that stood out. Perhaps it was his story, his gritty triumph over impossible odds. Or maybe I was just maturing in my role as a founder. But it didn't really matter; I was satisfied. I realized in that moment that even if we didn't help another person, I was okay. All our staff could quit, our bank account could be liquidated by a Russian hacker, I could get hit by a bus and be rendered unable to work, and it would still be enough. Not that I didn't want to succeed more, but the rest was just icing and birthday candles. The cake had already been made and baked, and I was at peace.

One of the secrets to living well in The Active Tension is defining early what success means to you and then living laser focused in response to your own definition. I wish I had learned this much earlier in my career. In recent years, I've let others dictate what success looked like *for me*, and in the pursuit of other's expectations, I stacked mountains of unnecessary pain and anxiety upon myself.

Even worse is if you let the culture at large decide what your success means. If this is where you are, you will never be satisfied. In pursuit of this ever-moving target, you may sacrifice relationships and risk burnout only to find your goals are still an arm's length away. In your next moment of clarity, think intently on what "enough" looks like for you. Consider writing it down even. Define your success as a person made for these times, and set a realistic target for when you hope to achieve it. Not only will you have a clearer path of where to go next, but once you reach the place you've already defined, you'll know real fulfillment.

But what if we can't meet a goal or live up to our own standard? This goes back to our pursuit of character and faithful identity. Success isn't just hitting a goal, or impacting one life or one million; it's actually resting in the knowledge that you are good enough no matter what. Our materialistic culture keeps us dissatisfied with what we have and who we are. We are always hungry for more and more. It takes great spiritual discipline to believe the identity God has already granted us and be content with who we are regardless. The greatest success we can find is the gift of truly knowing ourselves and being at peace with what we find.

Chapter 22

I'M GOING TO SLEEP

*Have courage for the great sorrows of life
and patience for the small ones; and
when you have laboriously accomplished
your daily task, go to sleep in peace. God
is awake.*

———

VICTOR HUGO

I read that Apple CEO Tim Cook wakes up at 3:45 a.m. every morning. He does some emailing from his home office, then goes to the gym, then to a coffee shop for more emailing, then to his office by 9:00 a.m. for the actual work. Sheesh. I suppose that's what you have to do when running a company with more money in the bank than the US Federal Reserve.

While I respect Tim Cook and enjoy Apple products, I can't for the life of me see how a schedule like that is sustainable. Most important, there seems to be little room for one's "private world." Popularized by Gordon MacDonald and his book *Ordering Your Private World*, our private world is the world outside of work. It's the time for family, gardening, walking in the woods, and lounging in sweats in front of the television. Our private world is a world of rest, reflection, play, and Sabbath. If we want to have an impact on our entire lives, we must order our private world.

From Gordon MacDonald:

> There is a temptation to give imbalanced attention to our public worlds at the expense of the private—more programs, more meetings, more learning, more relationships, more busyness. Until it all becomes so heavy that we teeter on the verge of collapse. Fatigue, disillusionment, failure, and defeat all become frightening possibilities.[1]

Ordering your private world means scheduling rest and reflection in the same way you schedule and prioritize work events. To order your private world is to tell the rest of us that you're in it for the long haul, that you're not going away. You won't get burned out. You're here to outlast all of us. Most important, ordering your private world is the intimate connection to the Creator. To stray too far into a public world disconnects you from the life force that put you here in the first place. Our private world should radiate influence to the outside world, rather than letting the outside world influence the deepest parts of us.

This is about biochemistry as much as spirituality. As Tony Schwartz notes, "Physicists understand energy as the capacity to do work. Like time, energy is finite, but unlike time, it is renewable."[2] Yet taking more time off is a foreign concept for many of us.

I recently came across three images posted online of people celebrated by their companies for prioritizing their work above all else.

The first is from Lyft, the ridesharing company, which highlighted Mary in Chicago with the "Golden Fistbump": "Shoutout to all the impressive Lyft parents out there—like Mary. A longtime Lyft driver who was still on the road at nine months pregnant. When contractions persisted, she headed to the hospital, but not before accepting one last request! The next morning, baby Maven Mia joined the Lyft family."

The second is an image and a quote with the CEO of Pair, a mobile app that lets you place images of home furnishings into a photo of a room in your home to see if you like the look before purchasing. Sounds pretty cool, until I saw an image and quote from their CEO: "I rarely get to see my kids. That's a risk you have to take."

Last is one from the mobile app Fiverr. The picture is of a young woman, with the green Fiverr logo below. The text reads, "You eat coffee for lunch. You follow through on your follow through. Sleep deprivation is your drug of choice. You might be a doer."

These three are celebrated examples of people putting their personal health and families at risk for the sake of their work. Not only is this type of behavior damaging for our bodies, but it's even more dangerous for our souls.

Reflected upon by Rev. Justin Schroeder, in his book, *Sabbath*, Wayne Muller writes of a South American tribe on a long journey. Hiking day after day, all of a sudden they would stop walking, sit down to rest, and then make camp for a couple of days before going any further. Even if they weren't tired or in an ideal camping location, the tribe explained that they "needed the time of rest so that their souls could catch up with them."

What a powerful image this is: stopping to rest so that their souls could catch up with them. Resting so that our head, heart, and soul can arrive in the same place, at the same time, in some kind of holy alignment.[3]

In a world of busyness and blur, I sometimes feel my soul is light years behind my mind and body. I think of the twenty-plus years of formal education and the thousands of hours of sports and exercise, and it's embarrassing to realize how many hours I've put into training my mind and body compared to how little I've put into training my soul. As I've learned through my own journey, our souls can only catch up with our bodies when we force ourselves to truly rest.

But rest is a unique concept all its own. For our honeymoon, my wife and I splurged on a fantastic all-inclusive resort in Cabo San Lucas, Mexico. We read by the pool, snorkeled in the ocean, exercised, ate nachos at 2:00 a.m., and slept in as long as we wanted. We booked a ten-day experience, but by about day five, I was restless. I'd finished the books I brought, and while my body was rested and semi-tanned, my soul wasn't at peace. I was eager to "do something," to build, to create. We often think of the best way to rest as just sitting on a beach somewhere, as far away as possible from our nine-to-five. But that isn't actually true. Leisure isn't the same as rest. As Chuck DeGroat explains, "The antidote to exhaustion isn't necessarily rest, it's wholeheartedness."[4]

Wholeheartedness is living in the reflection of our inner light. It's our deepest connection to the Creator, figuring out who we really are in order to become who we were made to be. Wholeheartedness is the way in which we "let go of what we thought we needed in order to experience what we already have."[5] It is here where we find true rejuvenation.

I've heard it said that those who work with their hands must rest with their minds, and those who work with their minds must rest with their hands. This means those of us who work with our hands all day can find rest in intellectual stimulation, while those whose work is primarily between their ears can find rest through physical exertion. My mentor Kevin recalled how he once took a week off of work to paint his house. He worked ten-hour days in the blistering sun, dangling from ladders and covered in paint. He concluded it was the most restful week of his entire life. He returned to work the next Monday with more energy than he could ever remember having.

On days when I need to rest, rather than lying down, the best thing I can do is leave my house and just run for as long as I can. I run until it hurts and see where God leads me. While I'm running, I always think of that line from *Fight Club* where Chuck Palahniuk writes, "I ran. I ran until my muscles burned and my veins pumped battery acid. Then I ran some more."

I run to escape how hard this road can be: the responsibilities of work, relationships, credit cards, and a mortgage. Some days I want to run all the way back to my hometown, all 850 miles, with each step transforming me younger and younger. Eventually I can arrive safely at my parents' house as a five-year-old boy without a care in the world. It would be a chance to avoid pain, to be taken care of once again, to stop.

One autumn day when I needed to rest and clear my head, I ran along Portland's leaf-covered sidewalks for as long as I could. Doubled over with exhaustion near the North Portland library, a street light flickered on above, and there stood my shadow. It was miraculously disconnected from my body, which was now illuminated in the light. In the yellow of the artificial glow, my shadow out of reach, I remembered who I was. Born in the image of God. Made for these times. Called to build and inspire, empathize, and laugh. Joy. I felt joy.

Suddenly I ran not to escape but to be free. I ran as a liberated ray of light, fused like a bolt of lightning to the heavens. My lungs expanded oxygen in abundance; I could do this forever. Time melted away. Finally slowing down back in front of my house, my shadow side of doubt and insecurity reconnected itself once more. But it was fainter and smaller, more of an opaque gray than a ghastly black. It was muted and manageable. I was renewed to fight another day. One more step toward wholeheartedness.

You cannot do everything. Yet so many of us are determined to do just that. We can schedule and plan and organize our lives exactly how we think they are meant to be lived, but the reality is that there is no such thing as perfect balance. Too many priorities pull for our attention.

Cardinal Dannels, the retired Archbishop of Brussels, Belgium, reminds us,

> When I get home after a long day, I go to the chapel and pray. I say to the Lord, "There it is for today, things are finished. Now let's be serious, is this diocese mine or yours?" The Lord says, "What do you think?" I answer, "I think it

is yours." "That is true," the Lord says, "it is mine." And so I say, "Listen, Lord, it is your turn to take responsibility for and direct the diocese. I'm going to sleep."[6]

The final four words of that quote have never left me: I'm. Going. To. Sleep. This is the daily life of admitting we need God. It's about giving our work over to the Lord for him to direct while we sleep.

In your pursuit of purpose, burnout and exhaustion follow closely behind, a dark passenger on your quest. All the momentum you've gained being made for these times is no more at risk than when you're tired and overwhelmed. It's here that you start making poor decisions and alienating the ones closest to you. You need to rest.

The first part of learning to rest is becoming more disciplined ourselves. This is where we schedule rest into our work calendars and map out special spots away from our homes or jobs where we go to meet God, the places where you'll leave your phone in the car and sit on a rickety bench overlooking a quiet park or a city skyline. It can be thirty minutes or three hours, but it is here where you're completely vulnerable, revealing your true self and allowing your soul to catch up with your body.

The second part is resting in such a way that we give over our busy lives to the Lord, like Cardinal Dannels entrusting the work of his diocese for God to manage while he sleeps. Rooted in the foundations of faith, Alcoholics Anonymous members recite *the Serenity Prayer*, reminding us to "accept the things we cannot change." Like a deep exhale of breath, we'll trust God to direct our lives while we sleep and accept the things we cannot change. It is here we'll find the strength to tackle tomorrow.

THIS ISN'T ABOUT

YOU.

IT NEVER WAS,

and wasn't meant

TO BE...

Part VI | THE COMMISSIONING

Despite the momentum, at many points along your journey, there will be times when you're ready to give in and give up.

The Resistance will have its boot on your neck, and you'll start to believe there is just too much evil in the world and too many dark forces at play, with most of the people you know too concerned with staying safe, soft, and content. You'll feel alone, and you'll say to yourself, *Things will never change, so why should I even try?*

In those moments, let me remind you of what a dear friend once reminded me. He dragged me back from the brink with these wise words: "Don't doubt in the dark what was inspired in the light."

While I believe God speaks to us in pivotal moments,

much of our success demands the ability to recall and remind ourselves of those moments when all hope feels lost. We must never allow an ember of an idea, stoked by elation and momentum, to be smothered by self-doubt in times of despair.

I meet many people at the beginning of their journey who share stories of late-night inspiration only to awaken the next morning with their vision a distant memory. Scared, anxious, overwhelmed, and insecure, they face an ounce of resistance and stamp out the smoke before it has a chance to catch fire.

We stifle those sparks of genius when we fear that we alone must start and sustain the fire, when we think it's all about us. But it's not. It's about God. I've nearly abandoned all I had worked for because I believed the vision was about me.

Now I know better.

Chapter 23

ROMERO TO THE RESCUE

In the top drawer of my office desk is a prayer about Archbishop Oscar Romero of El Salvador. During the gruesome years of the Salvadoran civil war, Romero was a moral force for the balance of spiritual devotion and seeking justice for the oppressed. Days after denouncing the government for human rights abuses, while in the middle of delivering mass, the peaceful archbishop took an assassin's bullet for his unyielding commitment to the poor. Most days, I don't begin work without reading a few lines of the prayer written about the martyred archbishop, "A Step Along the Way."[1]

> It helps now and then to step back and take a long view.
> The Kingdom is not only beyond our efforts, it is
> beyond our vision.
> We accomplish in our lifetime only a fraction of the
> magnificent enterprise that is God's work.
> Nothing we do is complete, which is another way of

saying that the Kingdom always lies beyond us.

We plant the seeds that one day will grow.

We water the seeds already planted knowing that they
hold future promise.

We lay foundations that will need further
development.

We provide yeast that produces effects far beyond our
capabilities.

We cannot do everything, and there is a sense of
liberation in realizing this.

This enables us to do something, and to do it very well.

It may be incomplete, but it is a beginning,

a step along the way, an opportunity for the Lord's
grace to enter and do the rest.

We may never see the end results, but that is the
difference between the master builder and the worker.

We are workers, not master builders; ministers, not
messiahs.

We are prophets of a future not our own.

Days before his death, Romero told a reporter, "You can
tell the people that if they succeed in killing me, that I forgive
and bless those who do it. Hopefully, they will realize they are
wasting their time. A bishop will die, but the Church of God,
which is the people, will never perish."[2]

To this day, his graffitied image paints the walls of San
Salvador, and his spiritual contributions to the Latin American
church reaches far beyond his years. Romero preached about
how our most successful contributions to the world lie in our
ability to act in vibrant recognition of our own imperfections.

Our shortcomings are not only normal but purposeful. We are meant to be broken and unfinished, waiting for God to invite us alongside him and achieve what he started well before us.

For those of us who are made for these times, one of the hardest things about doing work that matters is bearing the weight of it over time. It's a self-inflicted weight, one we've placed there ourselves. In our modern times, we can allow so much of our self-worth to be based on Western, capitalistic values of ambition, scale, and success. No matter how hard we work, we can rationalize how it's never enough. For so many of us, the nagging sense of responsibility and perfection is a blaring siren in the back of our minds. As a result, we lead lives of anxious toil, refusing to rest, rarely celebrating a job well done.

While our minds swirl with the anxiety of responsibility, the Romero prayer reminds us that we cannot do everything in our short time on earth. The foundations you lay will be shaky and need development. The seeds you plant will need more water than you are able to provide. Your accomplishments will be multiplied by others long after you are gone. And that's exactly the way it's meant to be.

It took me years to fully comprehend my relative smallness next to God's great vastness. This understanding frees us to do something small and to do it well. Our calling to the small things is the great invitation from the light that the darkness cannot overtake. This is liberation. We are liberated when we understand we are meant to do incomplete work. It is meant to not be enough. There will be loose threads, unfinished business, and entire pieces missing, but this is the way it was meant to be. God prefers our efforts to be unfinished because it allows him to bring in others who will pick up where we left off. You cannot do everything.

I envision the work of the Lord as gigantic heavenly wheels rotating all over the earth. They roll around scrubbing up the darkness, mowing down injustice, and building up shaky structures of redemption and renewal. Put in motion centuries ago, the wheels are relentless vessels of creativity and disruption. The greatest opportunities of our lives are when we are invited to ride on the wheels for certain seasons. We may join with God for one or two rotations, and then shift off so others can hop on when our time is up.

The end of the Romero prayer is my favorite. It proclaims that we are just the workers and not the master builder. If God is the foreman who casts the vision, we must allow him to mark the spots we're meant to dig and line up the seeds we are meant to plant. This isn't disparaging; this is liberation. Understanding our smallness as "just the worker" removes the crushing weight of human and cultural responsibility. We can take comfort in just showing up and putting our hand to the plow.

Even more liberating is when we comprehend that what we do today builds off the work of others in our past. Throughout God's grand redemption of humanity, every generation, if they choose to believe it, has been made for these times. Oscar Romero took a dramatic stand, knowing it would get him killed. As he predicted, even in death, God has used his work to live well beyond him. Nearly forty years later, a common phrase in El Salvador is *Romero vive* ("Romero lives"); he's become an inspiration for the countless others who follow in his footsteps. His work continues beyond the grave.

The story of Oscar Romero and the prayer about his legacy

has seen me through some of the darkest times of my life. The acknowledgment of his work being incomplete has made it possible for me to believe the same about mine. The peace this has brought has given me the opportunity to share it with you. I hope you'll take it to heart. The incomplete work of the past lives on, inspiring the next generation and the next. It enables ordinary people like you and me to make small and faithful contributions, knowing others are made for these times too.

Chapter 24

THE MIRACLE WORKER

Helen Keller was born both blind and deaf. As a young girl, she lived the beginning of her life in near total isolation. Without the ability to see a tree or hear what it was called, for a young Helen Keller, a tree didn't really exist. It was simply an immovable object obstructing her path. This inability to grasp that objects have names and purposes left her in a state of near total darkness, both physically and mentally.

The Helen Keller many people know is Helen Keller the global icon: the first deafblind person to graduate from college, writer, political activist, and lecturer. Most wouldn't know her as the scared little girl unable to make the connection between words, objects, and meaning. So how did a scared little girl go from a life of near total isolation to one of international recognition? Her ability to overcome such enormous obstacles was due in part to the tireless work of her teacher, Anne Sullivan. In her work with Anne, a moment stands out that changed everything—a moment that forever shaped a young Helen Keller and the lives of deafblind people for generations.

Here's the story, paraphrased from Robert Inchausti's book *Subversive Orthodoxy* and the play *The Miracle Worker*:

Anne Sullivan had joined Helen's family for dinner in their home to celebrate a successful two weeks of intense language training between Anne and Helen. While Helen's father was thrilled to see Anne has taught Helen basic table manners, Anne was still frustrated that Helen hadn't yet grasped the fundamental connection between signs and things.

Dinner had been going as planned, but then seven-year-old Helen made a mistake and dropped her napkin on the floor. Her mother had hoped to let the incident go unnoticed, but Anne was not going to let it slide. She demanded that Helen pick up her napkin. In an act of defiance, Helen swung her arm across the table, smashing the china and sending her mother's roast flying across the room. She then grabbed a pitcher of water and splashed it in Anne's face. The dinner was ruined, the progress of the last two weeks destroyed.

Taking Helen by the hand, Anne dragged her outside and forced her to refill the pitcher at the water pump. As she had done a million times before, she signed into Helen's hand and placed her hand upon the signed object.

"Pump!" Anne shouted, clamping Helen's hands onto the pump handle and signing "P-U-M-P."

"Water!" she screamed, and thrusted Helen's hands under the cold water, signing "W-A-T-E-R."

Helen continued to resist—crying, kicking, pushing, and pulling away. Then, as instantly as it began, Helen's tantrum stopped. She became quiet, absorbed, perfectly still. Rapt with attention, she had finally made the connection between words and things, signs and experiences, and for the first time in her life she grasped the idea that things have names. Helen whispered, "Wa, Wa," and in that moment she was transformed from an organism in an environment to a self in the world.

What happened next is every bit as moving. Helen began running around the yard trying to touch everything she could, thirsty for the signs to describe her world. In this dramatic moment, Helen understands that she is not alone in her world.

"What's this?" Helen indicated, touching a post. "And this? And this? And this?"

Anne called out to Helen's parents: "Mr. and Mrs. Keller! Come! Come! Helen knows. She knows!"

Helen's parents emerged from the house and Helen touched their faces, signing their names—knowing them as part of her world for the first time. Then she stopped and touched Anne's face. Anne reached for her hands and signed out the word "T-E-A-C-H-E-R," and Helen finally knew whom to thank for pulling her out of her isolation.[1]

Anne Sullivan worked relentlessly for years to bridge Helen's gap between words and things, and yet the final leap into understanding took only a matter of seconds. In this historic moment, Helen's sphere of awareness multiplies exponentially from her own little bubble to a seemingly endless ocean of possibility. For the first time in her life, Helen goes on a quest for meaning. Can you imagine the joy of a young

Helen running around her yard, finally able to grasp a larger world outside of her? In the span of one evening she learned thirty new words and became the connected human she was born to be.

Very few of us will have life-altering moments like Helen Keller's. But we should use this example as a point of inspiration for what our lives could become. Are you in a bubble? Has your sphere of awareness been limited primarily to yourself? Perhaps our role in the world is not just to wake up, work, buy stuff, feel safe, sleep, and do it all over again. What would happen if you opened yourself up to the possibility that you are connected to something far greater?

Everything changes when we realize our destiny is to accept the invitation from God to partner with him and to go out, create, build, and use our skills and abilities to work on behalf of our fellow human beings. Oh, the joy this brings! Like it was for Helen Keller, this is a messianic moment, a "scales off the eyes" revelation.

Regardless of your spirituality, political beliefs, or culture of origin, this invitation to cosmic human connectedness is one that no other species on earth gets to share in. So, will you take that leap? Will you allow yourself to grasp for a greater understanding? This is what it means to be made for these times.

———

Author and educator Parker Palmer wrote this great little book called *Let Your Life Speak*. It's the kind of book that finds you at the exact right moment, like discovering a crumpled up ten-dollar bill in an old jacket pocket while on your way to lunch.

Palmer argues it's impossible to go out and *find* who you are—it's something already deep within you. You find who you were meant to be by going inward. "Vocation does not come from a voice 'out there' calling me to something I am not. It comes from a voice 'in here' calling me to be the person I was born to be, to fulfill the original selfhood given me at birth by God."[2]

Most of us are scared of what we'll find, so we busy ourselves and jump from one activity to the next, never stopping long enough to meet our true selves face to face.

Palmer likens your purpose in life to a river that is flowing swiftly but frozen on the surface by an impenetrable sheet of ice. There you are, standing on top of the ice, trying to figure out the way to break through and fall into your "true life," the one God intended for you.

Our human nature is to wildly bash at the frozen cement with anything we can find, trusting the tools of the outside world. However, the best course of action is actually the exact opposite. To melt the ice, we need to slow down and listen, search the deepest part of our being, and let the searing heat come from inside us. This heat of self-awareness, our spirituality, the service to others, and our development of personal character will eventually thaw the ice and plunge us into the flowing river of the life we were meant to live.

At an earlier stage in my life, I read the river metaphor for finding our life's purpose and scoffed at its impracticality. Who would knowingly plunge themselves into an icy river? Stay on the surface, man! You will die. But years later, when I needed it most, this concept rang truer than it ever had before.

Maybe you're like me. You're roaming the earth trying to

figure out who you are, where you fit, and how to find meaning in the life you've been handed. In our desperation, we'll use whatever earthly tool necessary to pound at the ice, all the while forgetting that it's only the heat of our own soul, our 98.6-degree beating heart, that holds the answers.

The word *vocation* comes from the Latin word for "voice," a voice we must ensure we have ears to hear. Palmer writes, "Vocation does not mean a goal that I pursue. It means a calling that I hear. Before I can tell my life what I want to do with it, I must listen to my life telling me who I am."[3]

You first listen to discern if you are indeed made for these times. Here's a hint: you are. But it's now up to you to discover how you will apply it. You must continue to listen and search the deepest parts of your being. But the day will come when you truly understand *why* it is you've been made for these times. You'll realize it's been there all along, waiting for you. On that day, it will unlock the fire already within you, and the ice will begin to melt.

Chapter 25

THE CUSTODIAN

Hold everything in your hands lightly,
otherwise it hurts when God pries your
fingers open.

———

CORRIE TEN BOOM

Similar to a sugar high, when our work becomes a part of us and central to our identity, the early stages are fantastic. We can work harder, last longer, and dig deeper. My high lasted quite a long time. Multiple years, actually. Passion and grit layered with impact and hope. It was beautiful, and These Numbers Have Faces grew and grew. Then came the crash.

It's all very normal to feel responsible for the success or failure of something you start. But if we're not careful, this responsibility can derail into unhealthy levels of ownership. Suddenly the thing we've started, as noble as it may be, is "mine, all mine."

I've been blessed to be a part of an entrepreneurship community called Praxis. Based in New York, they equip and resource faith-motivated entrepreneurs who have committed their lives to cultural and social impact. Founders Dave Blanchard and Josh Kwan were the first to explain the difference between the *King* and the *Custodian* to me.

The King can do whatever he or she wants. With *King* as the root word in "Kingdom," all of it belongs to the King. Everything as far as the eye can see is his. Being the King is nice until you realize the things you own end up owning you.

Standing opposite the King is the Custodian. The Custodian sees the guardianship of an idea, mission, or enterprise both as temporary and as a precious gift. It does not belong to her, but instead she has an opportunity to steward it for a certain time and place.

As Josh Kwan writes in the *Praxis Journal,*

> In the Catholic order founded by Saint Francis of Assisi, the person responsible for the well-being of a province and the preservation of holy places is called a custos. This is where we derive our English words "custodian" and "guardian." St. Francis, ever the humble servant, chose for the leaders of his Catholic order a title that did not signify importance, but rather a set of responsibilities — to take care, to watch, to look after.[1]

Without a doubt, one of the greatest challenges of my adult

life has been surrendering These Numbers Have Faces and shifting my mindset from that of a King to a Custodian. After ten years at the helm, would I be able to let go?

You don't have to be an entrepreneur to experience this tension. We'll make ourselves Kings of nearly everything we can. In doing so, many elements of our life become burdens, even the best things. Our jobs, relationships, hobbies, political beliefs, and finances become idols in themselves, too wrapped up with our own identity. When one suffers, we suffer. We grasp them far too tightly. Surrender is hard.

In his book *Wholeheartedness*, Chuck DeGroat reminded me of one of Jesus' most controversial demands from Luke 14. "If anyone comes to me and does not hate father and mother, wife and children, brothers and sisters—yes, even their own life—such a person cannot be my disciple. And whoever does not carry their cross and follow me cannot be my disciple" (vv. 26–27).

This verse used to bother me to no end. What does he mean I have to hate my parents, wife, and family? There is no way I'm doing that. But then I learned what he was actually saying. Jesus, as he often did, is speaking in hyperbole and commanding us that we have to let go and surrender even the things we love the most. Our identity can be found only in him. We are Custodians, not Kings. We have to cut the cord. This isn't a selfish God demanding our obedience for his own sake. It's also for us. He knows we will actually find freedom on the other side.

These Numbers Have Faces is a part of me, and I of it. But there was a season when it became clear I could hold it no longer. It didn't belong to me. The organization had grown to a place where I was no longer needed in the same capacity. After months of soul searching, I realized it was time for me to step away as CEO and hand the reins over to someone else. After a particularly gut-wrenching phone call with my brother, Ryan, I broke down on my front porch, heaving with tears as I grappled with the weight of my decision. It was as though I was giving this child, one I had raised from birth, back to God where it had belonged in the first place. While I would continue to stay involved and always be the founder, I had to allow others more talented than me to take it from here.

Even in the surrender, the pain didn't stop for months. I had cold sweats at night, lost weight from skipping meals, and went back on anti-anxiety medication to deal with the fallout. DeGroat writes that even in the freedom of letting go, we'll face withdrawal symptoms. "As we let go, we begin to feel the effects. Just as an addict goes through withdrawal when giving up a drug, so our surrender will produce emotional and physical symptoms. We may feel even more tired, sometimes nauseous, often sad, and almost always anxious."[2]

Behind it all was the ever-present voice of God saying, "You must let go. You must find your identity in me and me alone." I knew the truth, but I was still second-guessing my decision.

———

Seven days a week, gathered on the corner below our office building in southeast Portland are dozens of day laborers. Why they chose this corner is unbeknownst to me, but from nearly 6:00 a.m. to 6:00 p.m. every day, they wait for someone to drive by and hire them. When we first moved into that particular office, I hired a few of them to come help us move in furniture, paint the walls, and assemble IKEA desks. Since then, every day for years I walk by them and give a friendly nod on my way in and out.

For most of the guys, the work never comes. By about 3:00 p.m., half the guys are lying down drunk against a chain-link fence. There is a twinge of guilt when I walk by them each day. I'm heading up to my office to work and build on behalf of young Africans seven thousand miles away, but one hundred feet from my office doors are the poorest and most marginalized people in all of Portland. They sit down there waiting for a job, and when it doesn't come, they choose the bottle, just like yesterday and the day before that. I've always felt for these guys, wishing there was something I could do to help them. But it's obvious that what they want most of all is a stable income, a chance to work every day and feed their families.

Parking near my office and walking up, the familiar sight of the dozen or so day laborers came into view. As I was about to cross the street, from my right approached a young man wearing a black baseball hat with a flat brim. Seeing him, I immediately lumped him in with the day laborers a few hundred feet ahead of us.

As we began to cross the street together, he turned to me and said plainly, *"Smile. Have confidence in the decision you've already made."*

"Excuse me?" I replied.

"Have confidence in the decision you've already made. It's going to be okay."

I reached the other end of the street, turned to face him, and asked, *"How did you know that? Why are you saying this to me?"*

"Because I could tell by your face that you are dealing with a big decision. You're going over it again and again in your head. But have confidence in what you've already decided."

At this point, I was too stunned to speak, and I looked at him dumbly. I'm shocked that this twentysomething day laborer could possibly know what's going on with my life, let alone just walk up to me and say it flat out.

We continued walking together, and he began to wax philosophically. *"You know the words homicide, suicide, and genocide?"*

"Yes," I responded in a concerned tone.

"The root of those words is cide; it's from the Latin phrase that means 'finality,' or the end of something. When it's done, it's over and done with. Same goes for you. You've made your decision. It's done. Be confident in it."

We had now approached the group of day laborers. I proceeded toward the door of my office building, and I watched him fall into the crowd.

I sat down at my office desk stunned by what had just happened. Then it became all too clear. God had sent someone, be it an angel or just this guy he spoke through, to tell me once and for all what I needed to hear. I'd made my decision. I'd surrendered. And it was going to be okay. I walked over to the window of our office that faces the street to look for the young man. Naturally, he was nowhere to be seen.

Besides getting the confirmation I needed in the most dramatic of ways, what I love most about this story is the messenger God chose to share it with me. God's kingdom is upside down. The last shall be first, the meek inherit the earth, the powerless gain power, the poorest among us end with the most riches. In typical fashion, the God of the universe decided to speak to me on that day through the most marginalized person imaginable. A young day laborer, likely undocumented, sits outside waiting for work. When it doesn't come, he does anything he can to numb the pain. God didn't use the voice of a friend, an entrepreneur I admire, or even a pastor to speak to me that day. He used the person he knew would impact me the most.

Being made for these times means you believe you've been called for something special in this life. But we must never forget it is not you who is special; it is God in you. We are addicted to the concept of ownership, but your life's calling does not belong to you. The work does not belong to you. The results do not belong to you. Instead, your life is a daily surrender of all things to the Creator. Not only does this mean freedom, but as the Oscar Romero prayer reminds us, there will be others who will come to pick up where you have left off. The seeds you plant now will grow beyond you. You are the worker, not the master builder.

Chapter 26

WE NEED YOU

A few hundred years ago, there were really only a handful of jobs a person could actually do. In eighteenth-century Colonial Williamsburg, the capital of the Commonwealth of Virginia before the Revolutionary War, the main professions for working men were farmer, blacksmith, carpenter, shoemaker, gunsmith, and tavern keeper. The barber doubled as the surgeon, and the apothecary acted as pharmacist, doctor, dentist, and general storekeeper.[1] Talk about multi-tasking! Women, of course, were in charge of the home, carrying the burden of a time in history where 40 percent of all children died before the age of five.[2]

One hundred years later, by 1870, over 50 percent of the American population worked in agriculture.[3] While they battled through the grisly years of the Civil War, half of the American populace still worked the fields every day. Today, according to the US Census, Americans in agriculture make up less than 2 percent of the population.[4]

Author and surgeon Atul Gawande described a nineteenth-century operation in which a surgeon was trying to amputate his patient's leg. The surgeon succeeded at that but accidentally amputated his assistant's finger as well. Both died of a severe bacterial infection, and an onlooker died of shock. It is the only known medical procedure to have a 300 percent fatality rate.[5]

I share this bit of American history because I don't think we stress enough how incredibly fortunate we are to be living in these times, not only for the clear advancements in health, economics, and infrastructure, but also in terms of the pursuit of self-discovery, vocation, and calling. What a privilege it is to live long enough and in relative comfort to even *consider* the possibility of pursuing a life tailor made to our greatest strengths, ambitions, and abilities.

Now, this isn't just for Westerners or those in the global north. Thanks to skyrocketing improvements in global health, human rights, the empowerment of women, high-speed internet, and access to capital and credit, people around the world can operate beyond mere survival and contemplate what it would look like to discover their deepest meaning and purpose. This is a remarkable time to be alive! I believe we sometimes put off what we were made to do because we don't fully grasp the historical context. We don't understand the gravity of our circumstances or the true privilege of living at this moment in time.

In the 1960s, Professor George Gerbner coined the term *mean world syndrome* to describe a correlation between the amount of television one watches and the amount of fear of the world around them one harbors.[6] We often allow the overwhelmingly good news to be fiercely overshadowed by a potent but small percentage of bad news.

People who are made for these times don't fixate on the negative or listen to the fearmongering of the news around them. They do as Fred Rogers described when he was afraid of the outside world: "When I was a boy and I would see scary things in the news, my mother would say to me, 'Look for the helpers. You will always find people who are helping.'"[7]

You're a helper. In your own way, you aim to help make the world a better place. We need people just like you, people who are inspired and empowered to confront the most pressing challenges of our time. Your challenge may be local or global, in the halls of Congress or within the walls of your own home. But we desperately need you. I often think of the heroic French commoners from Le Chambon. Ordinary in every sense of the word, they embodied deep character, showed courage in the forests of fear, and skillfully balanced a deep spirituality with social action. It was them in the 1940s just like it is you today.

Whether it's disbelief or fear or just plain insecurity, so many of us balk at the notion that we are significant. With the weight of the world's problems threatening to overwhelm us, we've neglected our sacred calling. In our uncertainty, we've forgotten who we were made to be. So we keep our heads down, focusing on the failings of the past instead of rising up to meet the destiny we've been granted.

But that isn't your story. Yours is one far greater. You've been made perfectly for these times, and you're never going back. Trust me.

Now is the time when I pass the torch on to you. I hope by now you understand just how special you are. Your birth was not an accident, nor was your upbringing or your pain. All of it has been molded by a Creator who desperately loves you. He believes in you so much he's invited you to work alongside him. As Gary Haugen says, "God has a plan to help bring justice to the world—and his plan is us."[8]

I hope by now you have a sense of The Resistance you must fight, the grit you must grow, the relationships to forge, and the character to develop. As you go forth, I hope you'll be able to balance the challenges of this life and surrender them when you know your time is up.

I'm energized by the idea of parallel paths—people might not be on the same road, but they are clearly headed in a similar direction. As you finish this book, keep in mind that a parallel path is my invitation to you. As your guide, I'd love to help you in any way that I can.

Together we will find the courage to make a small but meaningful difference in the world. Side by side, on parallel paths, we will confront our insecurities, battle our demons, and boldly face a future unknown.

You are built for more, and most important, you are capable and ready to do work that matters. The Resistance is strong, but the grit God has placed within you is stronger. And just as he called and equipped the heroes that have shaped history before us, he calls and equips you today. You were made for this, and now is your time.

"PEOPLE ARE STILL

GOOD,

MOSTLY," SHE SAID.

"Not from what I'm hearing,"

HE SAID.

"LOVE

IS QUIETER THAN GUNSHOTS.

BUT THERE'S

more of it."

ANONYMOUS

THANKS . . .

I'm so grateful for . . .

My beautiful wife, Trisha, who has journeyed alongside me through seasons of joy and pain. She was the first to support my crazy idea of starting a global education organization and has never wavered in helping me pursue work that matters. She's my final and most important editor, and I'm so thankful for the hours she spent enhancing this book. Her humor, love, and endless dance moves provide more life than I can begin to describe.

My daughter, Josephine, who has no idea how much our fun times at the park or cuddling on the couch have meant to me. I love being your dad.

My mom, dad, brother Ryan, Dave, Keana, along with Abraham and Estrellita Balicanta, who have been an incredible support to me as a husband, father, and entrepreneur. I'm so blessed to have a family who cares most about me being my very best self. My family was fundamental in the launching of These Numbers Have Faces and the completion of this book. What a gift to do the things you love alongside the people who love you the most.

The mentors throughout my life. Their investment in me is the ripple effect into the lives of others: Chris Cameron, Curtis Bronzan, Dana Sanders, Michele Mollkoy, Julie Degraw, Ken and Gail Heffner, Steve Stockman, Ken Humphrey, Clark Blakeman, Alan Hotchkiss, Darren Ho, Kevin Whitman, Lou Radja.

Everyone at These Numbers Have Faces, from the very beginning to today. Our courageous staff, board of directors, advisors, volunteers, interns, and faithful supporters. Thank you for taking my little vision and making it a part of your life too. Of course I can't forget our African students and entrepreneurs, whose bravery and grit are the manifestation of faith in action.

The stellar team at DC Jacobson and HarperCollins/ Zondervan. To Don and Blair Jacobson, who empowered me to write this book, along with Marty Raz, Laurel Boruck, Stephanie Smith, Brandon Henderson, and Robert Hudson.

Chris Palmer, the man most like me in nearly all ways, who has become a dear friend through this writing process, even though we've only actually hung out three times in real life.

Andy Jelderks, who stands and sings with me at every Portland Timbers home match. Through the sideways rain and blazing heat, he knows all too well how those ninety minutes are renewal for my soul.

Most important, to the God who continues to pursue me through the noise, meet me in the darkness, and invite me into adventure. Give me the ears to hear you.

Lastly, to you. Yes, you. I hope we can meet one day so I can hear about the ways you've been made for these times.

NOTES

Chapter 2: Starry Starry Night

1. Brenden Busse, "Andrew Garfield Played a Jesuit in *Silence*, but He Didn't Expect to Fall in Love with Jesus," *America: The Jesuit Review of Faith & Culture*, January 23, 2017, www .americamagazine.org/arts-culture/2017/01/10/andrew-garfield -played-jesuit-silence-he-didnt-expect-fall-love-jesus.

2. "Your Smartphone Is Millions of Times More Powerful Than All of NASA's Combined Computing in 1969," ZME Science, last modified May 17, 2017, www.zmescience.com/research/ technology/smartphone-power-compared-to-apollo-432/.

3. Martin Luther King Jr., "Letter from Birmingham Jail," April 16, 1963, Martin Luther King Research and Education Institute, okra.stanford.edu/transcription/document_images/ undecided/630416–019.pdf, 11.

Chapter 3: A Moment of Obligation

1. David Wilson, "College Graduates to Make Global Economy More Productive: Chart of the Day," Bloomberg, www.bloomberg.com/news/2010–05–18/

college-graduates-to-make-global-economy-more-productive
-chart-of-the-day.html/.

2. Laura Gilinsky, "Find Your Moment of Obligation," *Harvard Business Review*, April 15, 2013, hbr.org/2013/04/ find-your-moment-of-obligation.

3. "Goal: Reduce Child Mortality," UNICEF, www.unicef.org/ mdg/childmortality.html.

4. Shane Claiborne, *The Irresistible Revolution: Living as an Ordinary Radical* (Grand Rapids: Zondervan, 2006), 38.

5. King, *Letter from Birmingham Jail*, 2.

Chapter 4: The Conspiracy of Goodness

1. "Remember," Auschwitz, www.auschwitz.dk/Trocme.htm.

2. "Le-Chambon-Sur-Ligon," *Holocaust Encyclopedia*, United States Holocaust Museum, www.ushmm.org/wlc/en/article .php?ModuleId=10007518.

3. "Under the Wings of the Church: Protestant Pastor André Trocmé," *Yad Vashem*, www.yadvashem.org/yv/en/exhibitions/ righteous/trocme.asp.

4. Phillip P. Hallie, prelude to *Lest Innocent Blood Be Shed: The Story of the Village of Le Chambon and How Goodness Happened There* (New York: Harper Perennial, 1994), *xv*.

5. Hallie, *Lest Innocent Blood Be Shed*, 21.

6. David Brooks, "Everyone A Changemaker," The New York Times https://www.nytimes.com/2018/02/08/opinion/ changemaker-social-entrepreneur.html.

Chapter 5: Sandpaper

1. Daniel Pink, *Drive: The Surprising Truth About What Motivates Us* (New York: Penguin, 2009), 123–24.

2. Angela Duckworth, *Grit: The Power of Passion and Perseverance* (New York: Scribner, 2016).

Chapter 6: Hope Starts Here

1. Greg Boyle, *Tattoos on the Heart: The Power of Boundless Compassion* (New York: Simon & Schuster, 2010), 86.

Chapter 7: The Resistance

1. Steven Pressfield, *The War of Art: Break Through the Blocks and Win Your Inner Creative Battles* (New York: Grand Central, 2003), 63.

2. Ibid., 70.

3. Timothy Keller, in a Twitter posting: https://twitter.com/timkellernyc/status/848241052410630146.

4. Pressfield, *War of Art*, 39.

5. Sarah Collins, *Jesus Calling: Enjoying Peace in His Presence* (Nashville: Thomas Nelson, 2004), February 26.

6. Gary Younge, "Martin Luther King: The Story Behind His 'I Have a Dream' Speech," *The Guardian*, August 9, 2013, www.theguardian.com/world/2013/aug/09/martin-luther-king-dream-speech-history.

7. From a Twitter posting from the International Justice Mission, https://twitter.com/ijm/status/851238572678152192.

Chapter 8: Peak When You're Sixty

1. Rebecca J. Rosin, "The Moment When Nobel Prize Winner Peter Higgs Learned That His Particle Had Been Found," *The Atlantic*, October 8, 2013, www.theatlantic.com/technology/archive/2013/10/the-moment-when-nobel-prize-winner-peter-higgs-learned-that-his-particle-had-been-found/280389/.

Chapter 9: The Slow Work of God

1. Greg Boyle, *Tattoos on the Heart: The Power of Boundless Compassion* (New York: Simon & Schuster, 2010), 128.

Chapter 10: The Bonfire

1. Gustavo Gutiérrez, *A Theology of Liberation: History, Politics, and Salvation* (New York: Orbis, 1971).

2. C. S. Lewis, *The Lion, the Witch and the Wardrobe* (New York: Harper Collins, 1950) 80.

3. N. T. Wright, *Surprised by Hope* (New York: HarperOne, 2008), 132.

Chapter 11: Starve the Ego, Feed the Soul

1. David Brooks, "The Moral Bucket List," *New York Times*, April 12, 2015, www.nytimes.com/2015/04/12/opinion/sunday/david-brooks-the-moral-bucket-list.html.

2. Peter Walker, "Black Man Convinces 200 Ku Klux Klansmen to Leave White Supremacist Group by Befriending Them," *The Independent*, December 22, 2016, www.independent.co.uk/news/world/americas/kkk-klu-klux-klan-members-leave-black-man-racism-friends-convince-persuade-chicago-daryl-davis-a7489596.html.

3. Brooks, "Moral Bucket List."

Chapter 12: The Desire to Matter

1. Robert Inchausti, *Subversive Orthodoxy: Outlaws, Revolutionaries, and Other Christians in Disguise* (Grand Rapids: Brazos, 2005), 55.

2. Eric T. Wagner, "Five Reasons 8 out of 10 Businesses

Fail," *Forbes*, September 9, 2013, www.forbes.com/sites/
ericwagner/2013/09/12/five-reasons-8-out-of-10-businesses-fail/.

3. Caron Beesley, "Why a Mentor Is Key to Small Business
Growth and Survival," SBA.gov, www.sba.gov/blogs/
why-mentor-key-small-business-growth-and-survival-0.

4. UPS Pressroom, "The UPS Store Makes 'Mentoring Month'
Matter for Small Business Owners," www.theupsstore.com/
about/pressroom/small-business-mentoring-month-2014.

Chapter 13: You Can't Digitize Fishing

1. Thich Nhat Hanh, *Peace Is Every Step: The Path of Mindfulness
in Everyday Life* (New York: Bantam, 1991).

2. Katie Hafner, "Researchers Confront an Epidemic of
Loneliness," *New York Times*, September 5, 2016, www.nytimes
.com/2016/09/06/health/lonliness-aging-health-effects.html.

3. Jean M. Twenge, "Has the Smartphone Destroyed
a Generation?" *The Atlantic*, September 2017,
www.theatlantic.com/magazine/archive/2017/09/
has-the-smartphone-destroyed-a-generation/534198/.

4. Sarah Eberspacher, "Everything You Need to
Know About Japan's Population Crisis," *The Week*,
January 11, 2014, theweek.com/articles/453219/
everything-need-know-about-japans-population-crisis.

Chapter 14: Bound Together

1. Kate Chappell, "For Amish Teens, 'Rumspringa' Is a Chance
to See the Outside World," *WNDU*, South Bend, Indiana, July
29, 2015, www.wndu.com/home/headlines/For-Amish-teens
-Rumspringa-is-a-chance-to-see-the-outside-world-319046461
.html.

2. Eric Owens, "Rumspringa! Troopers Bust Minivan Packed with Drinking, Smoking Amish Teens Going 110 MPH," *The Daily Caller*, May 24, 2016, dailycaller.com/2016/05/24/cops-bust-drinking-amish-teens-in-minivan-going-110-mph/.

3. Melanie Curtin, "This 75 Year Harvard Study Found the 1 Secret to Leading a Fulfilling Life," *Inc.*, www.inc.com/melanie-curtin/want-a-life-of-fulfillment-a-75-year-harvard-study-says-to-prioritize-this-one-t.html.

4. Lila Watson, United Nations Decade For Women Conference: Equality, Development, and Peace, Nairobi, Kenya, July 15–26, 1985.

Chapter 15: The Most Revolutionary of Emotions

1. William H. Herndon and Jesse W. Weik, *Herndon's Life of Lincoln* (New York: Bedford, Clarke, 1889), 63–64.

2. Olga Kazan, "How to Make the Narcissist in Your Life a Little Nicer," *The Atlantic*, June 3, 2014, www.theatlantic.com/health/archive/2014/06/how-to-make-the-narcissist-in-your-life-a-little-nicer/372072/.

Chapter 16: Lighthouse on a Hill

1. Maggie Fox, "One in 6 Americans Takes Antidepressant, Other Psychiatric Drugs-Study," *NBC News*, December 12, 2016, www.nbcnews.com/health/health-news/one-6-americans-take-antidepressants-other-psychiatric-drugs-n695141.

2. Sarah Medina, "Takunda Mavina, Drunk-Driving Teen, Is Forgiven by Victim's Family," *Huffington Post*, September 17, 2012, www.huffingtonpost.com/2012/09/14/takunda-mavima_n_1882492.html.

Chapter 17: *Guernica*

1. Jeremy Rifkin, *The Empathic Civilization: The Race to Global Consciousness in a World in Crisis* (New York: Penguin Books, 2009).

2. Mary Pipher, *Writing to Change the World* (New York: Penguin Books, 2006), 3.

Chapter 18: You Can't Build the Kingdom Without the King

1. Harvey Siefert and Lois Siefert, *Liberation of Life: Growth Exercises in Meditation and Action* (Nashville: Upper Room Books, 1976), 179–81.

2. Henri Nouwen, *Show Me the Way: Daily Lenten Readings* (New York: Crossroad, 1992), 156.

Chapter 19: The Rainbow Nation

1. Nelson Mandela, *Long Walk to Freedom: The Autobiography of Nelson Mandela* (New York: Back Bay, 1994), 378.

Chapter 22: I'm Going to Sleep

1. Gordon MacDonald, *Ordering Your Private World* (Nashville: Thomas Nelson, 2003), 15.

2. Tony Schwartz, "Relax! You'll be more productive." *The New York Times*, February 10, 2013, https://www.nytimes.com/2013/02/10opinion/sunday/relax-youll-be-more-productive.html.

3. Rev. Justin Schroeder, "Joining a Circle: Letting Your Soul Catch Up with Your Body," *The Well: A Unitarian Universalist Blog*, September 10, 2014, wellswedidnotdig.blogspot.com/2014/09/joining-circle-letting-your-soul-catch.html.

4. Chuck DeGroat, *Wholeheartedness: Busyness, Exhaustion, and Healing the Divided Self* (Grand Rapids: Eerdmans, 2016), 118.

5. DeGroat, *Wholeheartedness*, 135.

6. MacDonald, *Ordering Your Private World*, 62.

Chapter 23: Romero to the Rescue

1. Bishop Ken Untener of Saginaw, "*Archbishop Oscar Romero Prayer: A Step Along the Way*," www.usccb.org/prayer-and-worship/prayers-and-devotions/prayers/archbishop_romero_prayer.cfm.

2. Renny Golden, "Oscar Romero: Bishop of the Poor" *US Catholic*, http://www.uscatholic.org/culture/social-justice/2009/02/oscar-romero-bishop-poor.

Chapter 24: The Miracle Worker

1. Inchausti, *Subversive Orthodoxy*, 75.

2. Parker J. Palmer, *Let Your Life Speak: Listening to the Voice of Vocation* (San Francisco: Jossey-Bass, 2000), 10.

3. Palmer, *Let Your Life Speak*, 4.

Chapter 25: The Custodian

1. Josh Kwan, "Roles of the Redemptive Entrepreneur: Anthropologist, Custodian, Prophet," *Praxis Journal*, June 19, 2017, journal.praxislabs.org/roles-of-the-redemptive-entrepreneur-anthropologist-custodian-prophet-2d681c683a70.

2. DeGroat, *Wholeheartedness*, 138.

Chapter 26: We Need You

1. "Occupation and Trades of the Eighteenth Century," Colonial Williamsburg, www.history.org/history/teaching/trades.cfm.

2. "Child Mortality," Our World in Data, ourworldindata.org/
child-mortality/.

3. "Historical Timeline—Farmers & The Land," Growing a
Nation: The Story of American Agriculture, www.agclassroom
.org/gan/timeline/farmers_land.htm.

4. "Employment in Agriculture," The World Bank, data
.worldbank.org/indicator/SL.AGR.EMPL.ZS.

5. Fareed Zakaria, "2012 Harvard Commencement Address,"
Harvard Gazette, news.harvard.edu/gazette/story/2012/05/
text-of-fareed-zakarias-commencement-address/.

6. Gavin Davie, "Cultivation Theory," Mass Communication
Theory, masscommtheory.com/theory-overviews/
cultivation-theory/.

7. "Helping Children With Scary News", Public Broadcast
Service, http://www.pbs.org/parents/rogers/special/scarynews
-thoughts.html.

8. https://twitter.com/ijm/status/788114336476782593.